2000

MARY ANGELA SHAUGHNESSY, SCN, JD, PHD

A Primer on Law for Administrators and Boards, Commissions & Councils of Catholic Education

NATIONAL ASSOCIATION OF BOARDS OF CATHOLIC EDUCATION
OF THE NATIONAL CATHOLIC EDUCATIONAL ASSOCIATION

Editor: D. Michael Coombe
Cover and text design: Beatriz Ruiz

Copyright 2000
National Catholic Educational Association
1077 30th Street, NW, Suite 100
Washington, DC 20007-3852
www.ncea.org

ISBN 1-55-833-241-3

Dedication

To my mother, Corine Bratten Shaughnessy,
faithful wife, loving mother, daughter, sister,
friend, aunt, and grandmother.
Mom, this one is for you.
Love, your daughter,

Angie
January 2000

Table of Contents

Dedication iii

About the Author vii

Acknowledgements ix

Preface x

1 Structure and Purpose of
Catholic Education Boards 1

2 The Laws Affecting Catholic
Education in the United States 5

3 Tort Liability of Educational
Institutions 16

4 Duties and Rights of Employees 25

5 Duties and Responsibilities of
Board Members 32

6 Privacy and Reputation 39

7 Staff and Student Relationships 43

8 Keeping Student Confidences 47

9 Child Abuse 53

10   Sexual Harassment   58

11   Students with Special Needs   63

12   Extracurricular and Cocurricular Activities   71

13   Athletics   76

14   Personal Conduct of Professional Staff   81

15   Gangs   85

16   Copyright Law, Technology, and Cyberspace   88

17   Health Issues   95

18   Setting Safety Policy   101

19   Some Concluding Thoughts   108

Glossary of Terms   116

Notes   120

Bibliography   121

About the Author

Sister Mary Angela Shaughnessy

Sister Mary Angela Shaughnessy is a sister of Charity of Nazareth who has taught at all levels of Catholic education from elementary through graduate school. She served eight years as principal of a Catholic high school. Sister Mary Angela holds a bachelor's degree in English and a master's degree in education from Spalding University, a master's degree in English and a law degree from the University of Louisville, and a Ph.D. in educational administration and supervision from Boston College. Her research centers on the law as it affects private education and church ministry. She is the author of 20 texts on the topic of law and the Catholic Church.

Sister Mary Angela is a regular speaker at the NCEA conventions. Sister serves as adjunct professor in Boston College's Catholic School Leadership program and as visiting professor in the University of San Francisco's Institute for Catholic Educational Leadership. Currently, Sister Mary Angela is professor of education and university legal counsel at Spalding University, as well as consultant for legal concerns for the Office of Lifelong Formation and Education in Louisville. She is a member of the bar in the state of Kentucky.

In June 1997, U.S. Secretary of Education Richard Riley named Sister Mary Angela to a virtually unprecedented second term on the prestigious America Goes Back to School Steering Committee. In 1998, the secretary appointed Sister Mary Angela to the National Committee on Family and Religious Partnership in Education.

She is the recipient of numerous awards, including the NCEA secondary department award, and was named in 1997 as one of the 25 most influential persons in Catholic education over the past 25 years. In 1999, she received the O'Neil D'Amour Award for outstanding service to boards of Catholic education from the National Association of Boards of Catholic Education of the National Catholic Educational Association.

Acknowledgements

Writing texts for the National Catholic Educational Association (NCEA) is a labor of love for me. The NCEA is the organization that was willing to publish my first text and has published many others. This latest text is a complete revision of the 1988 *A Primer on School Law: A Guide for Board Members in Catholic Schools*,[1] and reflects the rightful places of religious education and youth ministry within Catholic education. I sincerely thank Regina Haney, executive director of the National Association of Boards of Catholic Education, for her belief in me and in this work. I also thank the many boards of Catholic education across the country whose members have encouraged and promoted my work.

As always, I thank family members and my religious sisters, the Sisters of Charity of Nazareth, for their support. Most especially, I thank Miriam Corcoran, SCN, who has given unfailing support as proofreader and editorial advisor for this text and for all my work.

I thank the many good friends and colleagues at Spalding University who offer their friendship as well as their support. No writer with a full-time university job can succeed in writing and publishing without the support of the university's president. The president of Spalding University, Dr. Thomas R. Oates, is a man of uncommon vision who challenges me and all of us at Spalding University to be the best persons, scholars, teachers, and contributors we can be. I am forever in his debt.

Finally, I thank you, the readers. May your board membership give you joy and a sense of doing God's work.

Mary Angela Shaughnessy, SCN, JD, PhD

Preface

Laws are continually changing. Religious schools and programs once enjoyed considerable independence from the laws that govern other educational institutions. This is no longer the case. Although church-related institutions still experience some degree of independence under the separation of church and state principle of the Constitution, laws and court decisions increasingly are affecting church-related educational institutions and programs and in the United States.

Members of the councils, commissions, and boards of Catholic education that make policy as well as the administrators who implement policy are increasingly coming under scrutiny by the legal system in this time when the numbers of lawsuits and accusations of wrongdoing are escalating dramatically. It is vital, therefore, for all persons who are involved in the governance of church-sponsored educational programs to understand the ways in which current laws apply to them and to their decisions. Even advisory boards, which recommend rather than enact policy, and therefore are not held legally accountable, have a moral and practical responsibility to know the possible legal consequences of their recommendations (or lack thereof) for the staff and students entrusted to their care. Teachers, too, should clearly understand the legal parameters and consequences of their behavior.

This book is a valuable resource for understanding the laws which impact those who govern church-related educational programs. It explains many complicated legal principles in a style that is clear, direct, and easy-to-read. Although written with Catholic schools and educational institutions in mind, much of the book applies to private schools as well as to educational institutions affiliated with other religious denominations.

The National Association of Boards of Catholic Education (NABE) is pleased to present this publication to the education community. As the component of the National Catholic Educational Association (NCEA) dedicated exclusively to supporting boards, councils, and commissions of Catholic education, NABE believes that these entities (whatever they are called and however they function) need to provide the best support possible for administrators. In turn, administrators need the variety and depth of support that is available only by gathering the gifts which God has distributed throughout the community. As one if its many services, NABE continually strives to keep its members informed of the current laws and legal trends affecting those who govern church-related institutions of learning. This book is part of that objective. Those in the broader educational community who are trying to better understand the current legal atmosphere in this country will also find the book valuable.

Sister Mary Angela Shaughnessy, SCN, J.D., Ph.D., was the logical person to undertake this enterprise. Her previous writings have illuminated the laws affecting many aspects of church-related education. In 1988 she wrote a 47-page publication titled *A Primer on School Law: A Guide for Board Members in Catholic Schools*. The current volume is not simply a revision of *A Primer*, it is more comprehensive in scope and it examines the latest changes and trends in both legislative law and case law.

Once again, Sister Mary Angela has combined her extensive experience with her comprehensive knowledge of the United States legal system to provide a practical guide for the new millennium.

The National Association of Boards of Catholic Education is grateful to Sister Mary Angela for this significant contribution to our ongoing support for all who invest so much of themselves in making Catholic schools and educational programs as safe and as effective as they can be. We are also grateful for the assistance of D. Michael Coombe who edited this publication.

Regina M. Haney　　　　　　　　*Thompson M. Faller*
Executive Director　　　　　　　*Advisory Committee Chairperson*

National Association of Boards of Catholic Education

1

Structure and Purpose of Catholic Education Boards

Catholic education boards have witnessed much change since their beginnings, and the new millennium promises new challenges. Many boards are constituted as boards with limited jurisdiction, but consultative (advisory) boards are most common. For the sake of consistency, the terms *consultative board* and *board with limited jurisdiction* will be used.

A *consultative board* generally is established by the pastor, religious community, or diocesan policy. This board has responsibilities for the development of policies. The pastor has the final authority to accept the recommendations of the consultative board. The consultative models would be most effective if the pastor, principal, and/or director of religious education (DRE) are members of the board and attend meetings regularly. This would help to ensure that the principle of collegiality is functioning. If the pastor and administrator are not in regular attendance, the board members could view themselves as functioning in a vacuum. If they regularly decide not to follow the decisions of the board, members could view their role as useless.

Thus, even though a consultative board is, strictly speaking, advisory, the school's or program's best interests would be served if the board is able to use a consensus model of decision making whenever possible. Consensus does not necessarily mean everyone agrees that a certain action is the best possible action or one's personal preference; rather, consensus means that all members have agreed to

1

support the decision for the sake of the school or program. For example, if a board member had sole responsibility for appointment, he or she might personally have selected a different principal or DRE than the one the board chose. Because other board members prefer a given candidate, however, the board member agrees to support that candidate. It is important to note that consensus does not mean that the minority agrees to go along with the majority; it means that all members can support a decision. Sometimes the majority will support the choice of the minority if it is clear that the minority, in good conscience, cannot support the action that the majority favors.

A *board with limited jurisdiction* has been defined as one "constituted by the pastor to govern the parish education program, subject to certain decisions which are reserved to the pastor and the bishop."[2] This type of board has, in both theory and practice, more autonomy in decision making than the consultative board, because the pastor has delegated this decision-making power to the board with limited jurisdiction. Pastors and bishops can delegate power, but they cannot delegate their ultimate responsibility for actions taken in their parishes or dioceses. The responsibility of superiors for the actions for those reporting to them has roots in civil law as well as in canon law. The civil law doctrine of *respondeat superior* requires that a superior must answer for the actions of a subordinate. Generally, for example, if a Catholic education board is sued for its actions, the pastor and the bishop will be sued as well.

Private schools owned by religious congregations or other bodies such as boards of trustees may have either consultative boards or boards with limited jurisdiction. The board of a school owned by a religious congregation would relate to the administrator of the religious congregation in the same manner as a parish school board would relate to a pastor. Since most boards are consultative and do not have final decision-making powers, board members will not ordinarily be liable for actions taken. Nonetheless, the parish or school should provide liability insurance for its board members, unless state law clearly indemnifies members of nonprofit boards from liability.

Some Catholic schools may utilize a corporate board type of structure, sometimes called a corporate board or a board of trustees. Those who operate the school incorporate under state law, and a corporate charter and bylaws are established. This corporate body would be the ultimate authority except in those areas reserved to the bishop.[3] Some Catholic schools and programs have a two-tiered board structure. In this type of structure, a member board would have ultimate authority but would delegate some decision-making powers to a lower board, such as a board of directors. Canon law requires that a school or program wishing to call itself Catholic have the permission and recognition of the bishop. Traditionally, a Catholic school must be subject to the bishop in matters of faith and morals. Canon law requires that the bishop exercise supervision over the religious education programs of schools and parishes and those who teach in such programs. Catholic schools and programs, as well as their board members, must therefore understand and accept the authority of the local bishop in these matters. To attempt to act in a manner contrary to the wishes of the bishop could place a school's or program's continuation at risk.

A growing number of traditionally Catholic schools have dropped the word "Catholic" from their official titles and have begun to call themselves, for example, "an independent school in the Catholic tradition." It is important for all involved in the governance and educational ministry of such an institution to understand that one cannot be both truly Catholic and completely independent. To be a Catholic school or other Catholic educational program requires that the authority of the bishop, as outlined in canon law, be recognized. Before making a decision to drop "Catholic" from a school's, or program's name, those responsible should thoroughly consider the ramifications.

Many consultative boards function like boards with limited jurisdiction. Government by collegiality and consensus sometimes results in little, if any, formal vote taking; therefore, in practice, it is often difficult to distinguish between consultative boards and boards with limited jurisdiction.

PURPOSE

Boards of education have an important role in the life of the institution. It is crucial that board members understand that power is vested in the board *as a body*, not in individual members. Board members must understand that the role of the board is the development of policy. Even if the policies have to be approved at a higher level, board members must understand their role in terms of policy.

Policy is usually defined as a guide for discretionary action. Thus, policy will dictate what the board wishes to be done. Policy is not concerned with administration or implementation, that is, the board should not become involved in *how* its directives will be implemented or with the specific *persons* who will implement them. For example, a board might state as a policy that students are to wear uniforms. The board would not be concerned with what company provides the uniforms or with what color they are. Similarly, the board might establish a policy requiring family participation in sacramental preparation. The board would not, however, determine the content of, or the time and place for, the programs. Such questions are administrative and are to be dealt with by the administrator, who is the chief executive officer of the school or program and also the chief executive officer of the board. Administrative decisions are the day-to-day management choices of the administrator. It is important for everyone to understand these distinctions from the beginning.

CIVIL LAW

Generally, boards will set policies in at least three major areas: program, finance, and personnel. The board may also have responsibility in the area of plant maintenance. Board members, therefore, need to know the broad parameters of the law as it affects Catholic education.

The purpose of this text is to provide prospective and current Catholic board members with basic information concerning civil law as it impacts education in general and Catholic schools and other Catholic educational programs in particular. A court would generally expect that a person who accepts membership on a board would have some rudimentary understanding of the laws that apply to that system.

REFLECTION QUESTIONS

1. If a parish member stops you at the front of the church one day and asks you what exactly the board does, how would you respond?

2. Give examples of policy decisions the board has made or recommended. How has the administrator implemented the decisions?

2

The Laws Affecting
Catholic Education
in the United States

The laws affecting education in the United States today generally can be classified in four categories: constitutional law (both state and federal constitutions), statutes and regulations, common law principles, and contract law.

Board members must understand that the law is not the same in the public and private sectors. Federal constitutional law protects individuals against the arbitrary deprivation of their constitutional freedoms by government and government officials. Constitutional law protects students and teachers in public schools since public schools are governmental agencies and the administrators of public schools are public officials.

Practically, this means that Catholic schools or other religious programs can have regulations and procedures that would not be permissible in a public school or program. Students can be required to wear uniforms; the expression of free speech can be limited. For example, students and teachers would probably not be allowed to wear buttons criticizing the pope or promoting abortion. Catholic institutions have a legal right to make these regulations. If public schools and programs attempted to impose similar rules, they could be guilty of violating the right to free speech as guaranteed by the First Amendment.

Education board members need this information. A parent, student, or teacher might claim that some constitutional right, such as free speech, had been violated. It is important for school board

members (and, indeed, for all involved with the school) to understand that a person does not have the same rights in a private setting
that one would have in a similar public setting. One can always
choose to leave the private setting, but as long as one chooses to stay,
the exercise of certain freedoms can be restricted. This does not
mean that a board can be arbitrary in developing policies. But
Catholic schools, religious education, and youth ministry programs
do not have to accept all the behaviors that the public sector must
accept.

CONSTITUTIONAL LAW

In only two situations can Catholic or other private institutions
be required to grant constitutional protections: 1) if state action can
be found to be so pervasive within the institution that the institution
can be considered a state agent, and/or 2) if a compelling state
interest, loosely defined as an overwhelming need for an action, can
be shown.

Some of the main arguments advanced to prove the presence of
state action in private educational institutions are: 1) an institution's
acceptance of government monies; 2) the tax-exempt status of the
private institution; 3) education as a quasi-state function (sometimes
called a "public benefit theory" since schools, particularly elementary
and secondary ones, perform a public service); and 4) state involvement with the school or program through accreditation or similar
procedures and/or statutory requirements with which the institution
complies.

A relevant case is *Rendell-Baker v. Kohn,* 102 S. Ct. 2764 (1982),
which involved a dismissed teacher in a private school that received
90-99% of its funding from the government. The United States
Supreme Court ruled that, despite the level of funding, there was no
state action in the school. Since the government had no role in
dismissal decisions, the school was not required to grant any constitutional protections to its teachers and, one might assume, to its
students. No student or teacher using a state action argument has
prevailed in a lawsuit against a private school or program to date. It
should be noted, however, that some attorneys and judges would like
to see constitutional law and program protection extended.

Given that private religious institutions and programs have the right to exist and are not bound to grant constitutional protections unless significant state action is found, litigants alleging a denial of constitutional rights will have to prove the existence of significant state action within the institution before the court will grant relief.

Cases indicate that without a finding of state action or compelling state interest, the courts will not hold Catholic schools or programs to the requirements of constitutional protections. The case law should not be interpreted to mean that Catholic schools and programs can do anything they wish and the courts will not intervene. Case law is constantly developing and so it is difficult to state hard and fast rules. The fact that no case involving student discipline in the private arena has ever reached the United States Supreme Court indicates, perhaps, the reluctance of the court to intervene in the private sector.

State constitutional law may apply to private as well as public institutions. It is not unusual to find a statement such as, "Anyone owning and operating an educational institution in this state shall...." So long as whatever is required does not unfairly impinge upon the rights of the private educational institution and can be shown to have some legitimate educational purpose, private schools and programs can be compelled to comply with the state constitutional requirements.

STATUTES AND REGULATIONS

Federal and state statutes and regulations govern public schools and institutions, and may govern religious institutions as well. Failure to comply with reasonable regulations can result in the imposition of sanctions. The case of *Bob Jones University v. United States*, 103 S. Ct. 2017 (1983), illustrates this point. Because of a religious belief, Bob Jones University's admissions and disciplinary policies are racially discriminatory. The Internal Revenue Service withdrew the university's tax-exempt status based on a 1970 regulation proscribing the granting of tax-exempt status to any institution which discriminated on the basis of race. Before a private institution will be forced to comply with a law or regulation, the state's compelling interest in the enforcement of the regulation will have to be shown. In this case, the government's compelling interest in racial equality was sufficient for the court to order Bob Jones University to comply with the anti-discrimination legislation or lose its tax-exempt status. In effect, the court said, "We cannot compel you to change your religious belief, but the government will not give you support in the form of tax-exempt status in order to advance this discriminatory belief."

The loss of tax-exempt status is no small matter. Such a loss would put most Catholic schools and programs out of business, since the institutions would not be able to pay the taxes that would be owed. *Dolter v. Wahlert,* 483 F. Supp. 266 (N.D. Iowa 1980), is similar to *Bob Jones.* A Catholic school was found guilty of sex discrimination when it did not renew the contract of an unmarried, pregnant teacher, since the evidence clearly indicated that unmarried male teachers who were known to have engaged in premarital sex were evaluated by a different standard.

Federal law prohibits discrimination on the basis of race, sex, handicap, age, and national origin. Although it also prohibits discrimination on the basis of religion or creed, the right of religious organizations to give preference to their own members is upheld. Practically, this means that Catholic schools may give preference to Catholic teachers and other employees. Board members must bear in mind that such preference must be stated in written policies.

The government cannot pass laws so restrictive that an institution's existence is placed in jeopardy. The right of the Catholic school to exist was firmly established by the Supreme Court in 1925 when a religious order operating a private school brought suit challenging an Oregon statute which would have made public education compulsory. In this landmark case, *Pierce v. the Society of Sisters,* 268 US 510 (1925), the Supreme Court declared the statute unconstitutional because it interfered with the rights of the school owners. The court also stated that it interfered with the rights of parents to choose the education of their children.

COMMON LAW

The third type of law, which applies to both public and private sectors, is the common law. *Black's Law Dictionary* (1979) defines common law:

> "Common Law" consists of those principles, usage and rules of action applicable to government and security of persons and property which

do not rest for their authority upon any express and positive declaration of the will of the legislature. Common law principles may also be derived from God's law, especially by persons in religious schools. Many common law principles are founded in basic morality, found in the Bible and in other religious writings. Due process or fairness considerations can be considered part of the common law. (p. 251)

In order to discuss common law considerations of fairness, one must understand the meaning of constitutional due process/fairness. There are two kinds of constitutional due process: procedural and substantive.

Much has been written about due process, but one of its simplest definitions is that of "fairness." One would expect that parties to a suit in court will be treated fairly by the judge and/or the jury. Similarly, one expects that a person accused of a crime will be told what it is he or she is accused of having done (notice); that he or she will be given a hearing or trail by an impartial party or parties; that the accused will be able to confront the accusers (cross-examination) and call witnesses on his or her own behalf. In a court case, one would also expect that an attorney would represent an accused person.

Substantive due process has been defined as meaning that "if a state is going to deprive a person of life, liberty or property, the state must have a valid objective and the means used must be reasonably calculated to achieve the objective."[4] Substantive due process involves moral as well as legal ramifications: Is this action fair and reasonable? In the public sector, substantive due process is present whenever a person has property (anything that can be owned, whether tangible or not) or liberty (freedom and/or reputation) interests.

In public school due process cases, justices have called for actions based on morality, as much as on what the Constitution does and does not demand. Courts rely on a belief that educators are trying to do what is right. Since educators are assumed to be behavioral models for students, courts hold educators, whether in public or private schools, to strict standards of fairness.

While Catholic schools and programs are not held to the Constitution, courts have indicated that they can be held to standards of fairness in accordance with the school's or program's principles and commonly accepted standards of reasonable behavior. In a case involving a dismissed Catholic school student, the court stated:

> A private school's disciplinary proceedings are not controlled by the due process clause, and accordingly such schools have broad discretion in making rules and setting up procedures for [their] enforcement, nevertheless, under its broad equitable powers a court will intervene where such discretion is abused or the proceedings do not comport with fundamental fairness. *Geraci v. St. Xavier High School,* 13 Ohio Op. 3d 146 (Ohio 1978)

The court suggests that, even if state action does not exist in private institutions, they may still be held to a standard of what it called "fundamental fairness." Fundamental fairness is sometimes used as a synonym for due process, although constitutional due process requires specific protections as stated in the law and interpreted by the courts. Fundamental fairness in the private setting, though similar to constitutional due process, should not be equated with it.

In a private school case similar to *Geraci, Wisch v. Sanford Schools, Inc.,* 420 F. Supp. 1310 (1976), the court scrutinized the school's rules and dissemination of its code of conduct to determine that what it called "contractual procedural fairness" had been given the student. The court specifically addressed the basic fairness provision in a private school-student relationship and stated that such fairness would have been better met if the school had had a written disciplinary code.

CONTRACT LAW

In the Catholic school or program, contract law is the predominant governing law. A contract may be defined as "An agreement between two or more persons which creates an obligation to do or not to do a particular thing" (*Black,* 1979, pp. 291-92). Generally, the five basic elements of a contract are: 1) mutual assent 2) by legally competent parties 3) for consideration 4) to subject matter that is legal and 5) in a form of agreement which is legal.

Mutual assent implies that two parties entering into a contract agree to its provisions. A Catholic school agrees to provide an education to a student and, in return, his or her parents accept that offer and assume certain obligations. A Catholic school offers a teacher a contract and the teacher accepts. A parish religious education program offers sacramental preparation to the family, and the family accepts. If one party does not or cannot agree to the terms of the contract, then no valid contract exists. Agreement is the first of five factors necessary for a valid contract.

Legally competent parties implies that the parties entering into the contract are lawfully qualified to make the agreement. A school or parish is legally qualified to enter into contracts to educate students and to employ teachers. Parents are legally competent to agree to pay tuition and meet other obligations. A properly qualified teacher is a legally competent party; a person who does not possess the qualifications needed to perform as a teacher would not be a legally competent party to enter into a teaching contract.

Consideration is what the first party agrees to do for the other party in exchange for something from the second party. The Catholic school agrees to provide educational services to a student in return for payment of tuition and adherence to the rules. The school agrees to pay the teacher a salary in return for teaching services. The parish offers a religious education program in return for parental support and perhaps payment of tuition or fees.

Legal subject matter assumes that the provisions of the contract are legal. An agreement as a condition of employment that a teacher would not marry a person of another race would not be legal, as such a condition would probably be construed as a violation of law, especially of antidiscrimination laws.

Legal form may vary from state to state. If a contract calls for witnesses, and no witnesses' signatures are found on the contract, then the contract is probably not in legal form. If any one of the five basic elements of a contract is missing, the contract may be held to be null and void.

Excluding allegations of negligence, cases against Catholic schools very often are breach of contract cases. The breach occurs when one party, with no good reason, fails to perform that which was promised. Breach of contract can be committed by any party to the contract (the school/administrator, teacher, or student). Most principals would agree that a most frustrating experience occurs when a teacher who has signed a contract breaches that contract to take a position in a public school. However, it is generally considered futile for a Catholic school to bring a breach of contract charge against a teacher who wants to terminate his or her contract, for it is highly unlikely that a judge will compel a person to teach against his or her wishes. Instead of requiring continued performance, it might be preferable to extract damages for breach of contract. The theory maintains that courts should not compel the performance of a contract if one of the parties does not wish to provide the service.

In a dated but still applicable Catholic school breach of contract case, *Weithoff v. St. Veronica School,* 210 N.W. 2d 108 (Mich. 1973), the court considered the case of a teacher who had been dismissed from her position because of her marriage to a priest before he was free to marry in the Catholic church. The court was careful to note that a church-sponsored school could contractually require teachers and other employees to observe the tenets of the sponsoring school's faith. The testimony showed that a regulation requiring teachers to be practicing Catholics had been adopted but was never promulgated. Since the teaching contract bound the employee to "promulgated" policies, the court held that the school could not legally dismiss the teacher. Obviously, if the regulation had been promulgated, the case might have had a different ending.

Another conclusion was reached in the similar case of *Steeber v. Benilde—St. Margaret's High School,* No. D.C. 739 378, Hennepin County, Minn. (1978) in which a teacher protested the nonrenewal of her contract following her remarriage after a civil divorce. The court upheld the right of the school to terminate the teacher's contract since she was no longer a member in good standing of the Catholic church.

In the first case, the school breached its contract with the teacher because it failed to promulgate the rule to which it sought to hold the teacher. In the second case, in a very similar situation, the court ruled in the school's favor because the school had properly proceeded according to the provisions of its contract. Issues of teacher lifestyle can pose serious problems for educational administrators and boards. These issues will be analyzed in greater detail later in this text. The bottom line in any discussion of administrator, teacher, or student rights is that no one possesses the same constitutional rights in the private sector as they would in the public sector. Thus, contract law and statutory laws are the main governing rules for private education.

Three private school student discipline cases illustrate that contract law places obligations on the institution as well as on the parents and students.

The 1981 case of *Bloch v. Hillel Torah North Suburban Day School*, 438 N.E. 2d 976, involved a first grader expelled in mid-year for excessive absence and tardiness. The parents alleged that the expulsion was in retaliation for the mother's actions in reporting a head lice epidemic to the health department. The parents charged that, according to usage and custom, the first year's contract required the school to provide eight years of education. The court ruled that the school was not bound to continue educating the child because of the highly personalized nature of the educational services. Relying on the principle that the remedy for breach of contract is damages not performance of the contract, the court ruled that the parents could seek financial damages from the school, not reinstatement.

This case demonstrates the fact that a private school or program, whether Catholic or nonsectarian, will not be forced to reinstate a wrongfully dismissed staff member or student. It is important for everyone in the Catholic educational setting to understand this fact. A court could, however, order the reinstatement of a wrongfully terminated public school student or teacher because of the requirements of the Constitution.

At first glance, this ability to employ and to accept whom one wishes might seem unfair. Our American system of private enterprise operates under a doctrine of "employ at will." No one can be compelled to remain in a private relationship that is repugnant to him or her. If terminating the relationship violates contractual agreements or basic fairness, the terminating party may have to pay damages in compensation but, at least to date, no private school has been ordered by a court to reinstate a student or teacher, regardless of the reason for dismissal.

Two previously cited cases also illustrate breach of contract. In the *Wisch* case, the court ruled that the school did not breach its contract by expelling the student who had violated school rules. In the *Geraci* case, which involved a student who helped a student from another high school obtain entrance to the school and throw a pie in a teacher's face, the court ruled that the student, not the school, had breached the contract.

The importance courts rightfully place on the development, promulgation, and implementation of rules is enormous. Since handbooks and other written agreements can be construed as part of the contract existing between the school/program and students and parents or between the school/program and teachers, it is important that as far as possible and practical, rules be in writing.

Courts will look for evidence of good faith: Did the institution have a rule? Was that rule promulgated, i.e., did the parties concerned—students, parents and teachers—know of the rule? Courts will generally not concern themselves with the wisdom of the rule— or even with the rightness or wrongness of the rule. The court is concerned only with the existence of a properly promulgated rule or policy and with evidence that the institution or program acted in good faith, according to the procedures it stated would be followed. Courts will look for basic fairness in the execution of the contract between the Catholic school/program and the student/parent or the teacher when it is alleged that the school or program acted improperly and so breached the contract.

Board members, then, should have at least a minimal understanding of civil law and its application to the private sector. At this point in time, the only occasion in which constitutional protections may be invoked in private schools is in the area of discrimination. Contract law and the provisions of the contract existing between the disputing parties will determine all other cases alleging deprivation of rights.

REFLECTION QUESTIONS

1. The board chair has just read a letter to the board and asked for the members' help in responding to the writer, a parent who has written to complain that his son was told to remove his eyebrow ring. According to the parent, the child's constitutional rights have been violated. How should the board chair respond to this letter?

2. The DRE asks the board's advice concerning an extremely belligerent, uncooperative parent who refuses to believe that her child could do anything wrong and who comes to the religious education program to scream and threaten staff members: "You will be sorry that you treated Leslie this way. Just remember when it happens that I warned you." The religious education program handbook discusses parental cooperation but stops short of stating that the ultimate penalty for lack of parental cooperation is dismissal of the child. The DRE tells the board that he is running out of patience but he hates to put the child out of the program when the child's behavior is no worse than other children's. What would you advise the DRE to do?

3

Tort Liability of
Educational Institutions

Tort law, a type of statutory law, is sometimes considered a fifth type of law. Civil lawsuits brought by teachers, parents, and/or students against schools or other institutions are often in the nature of tort suits. *Black's Law Dictionary* defines a tort as "[a] private or civil wrong or injury, other than breach of contract, for which the court will provide a remedy in the form of an action for damages" (p. 1335).

Black distinguishes between private torts and constitutional torts. If public sector officials were to be found guilty of a constitutional tort, such as a deprivation of due process or some other constitutionally protected right, they would be said to be acting under "color of law." Catholic school/program officials could not normally be guilty of a constitutional tort because they would not be acting as public officials.

Torts are one area in which public schools may seem to have more protection than Catholic schools and parishes. Under the doctrine of sovereign immunity, public officials are granted immunity from liability for torts that result from the performance of their official duties. The doctrine had its beginnings in English common law that did not permit anyone to sue the monarch without his or her consent. However, the reader should note that recent case law indicates a movement toward abolishing sovereign immunity.

This protection would not apply to a Catholic school or parish official, since such a person is not considered a state official. Churches and religious schools in some cases have successfully invoked an analogous doctrine of charitable immunity in the past. Both sovereign immunity and charitable immunity, although they are still appropriate legal defenses, have fallen on hard times. Judgments indicate that both government officials and charitable institutions are bound to exercise the same degree of care a mature, reasonable person or group of persons would exercise.

A public school case illustrates. In *Wood v. Strickland*, 420 U.S. 308, 95 S. Ct. 992 (1974), public school officials and school board members were held liable for their actions if they knew or should have known that their actions could or would result in the students' being deprived of their constitutional rights. Analogously, it seems reasonable to suppose that private school board members would not be allowed to take refuge under charitable immunity if they knew or should have known that their actions could result in harm to individuals.

Tort suits generally can be classified along four categories in schools and programs: 1) negligence, 2) corporal punishment, 3) search and seizure, and 4) defamation. Although students will most often bring suit under the first three categories, anyone injured on school or parish grounds may bring negligence suits. Defamation suits may be brought by students who seek to show wrongful expulsion or other disciplinary measures, but, more likely, teachers who are disciplined or who have their contracts terminated or not renewed will bring defamation suits.

NEGLIGENCE

Negligence continues to be the most common of all lawsuits filed against teachers, administrators, and others who supervise children and adolescents. Even though negligence is the "fault" against which schools/programs must constantly guard, it is also the most difficult type of case about which to predict an accurate judicial outcome. What may be considered negligence in one court may not be considered negligence in another. Obviously it is much better to avoid being accused of negligence in the first place than to take one's chances on the outcome of a lawsuit.

Gatti and Gatti have defined negligence as "the unintentional doing or not doing of something which wrongfully causes injury to another."[5] Four elements must be present before negligence, in the legal sense, can be said to exist. These elements, which have been defined by many legal writers, are: *duty, violation of duty, proximate cause*, and *injury*. If any one of the four elements is missing, no negligence and, hence, no tort can be found to exist. Since negligence is an unintentional act that results in an injury, a person charged with negligence is generally not going to face criminal charges or spend time in prison. If an injury is intentionally inflicted, the perpetrator has committed a criminal act of assault and battery. An examination of each of the four elements necessary to constitute a finding of negligence should be helpful.

Duty. The person charged with negligence must have had a duty in the situation. Students have a right to safety, and teachers and school officials have responsibilities to protect the safety of all those entrusted to their care. Boards are expected to develop policies and administrators are expected to develop rules and regulations which provide for the safety of all.

Board members and administrators should be aware that courts might hold them responsible for student behavior and its consequences occurring on school or parish property before or after school. Case law indicates that administrators can be held liable for accidents occurring on property before and after school or program hours.

In an early but important case, *Titus vs. Lindberg*, 228 A2d 65 (N.J. 1967), an administrator was found liable for student injury occurring on school grounds before school hours for the following reasons: he knew that students arrived on the grounds before the doors were opened; he was present on the campus when students were; he had established no rules for school conduct outside the building, nor had he provided for supervision of the students. The court found that he had a reasonable duty to provide supervision when he knew students were on the property and that students were there as a regular practice. Although there was no school board involved in this case, it is relatively easy to see how board members could be involved if a similar situation were to occur today.

Violation of duty. Negligence cannot exist if the person charged with negligence has not violated a duty. If a teacher is properly supervising a playground and one child picks up a rock, throws it and so injures another child, the teacher cannot be held liable. However, if a teacher who is responsible for the supervision of the playground were to ignore rock throwing or were to allow it to continue and injury resulted, the teacher probably would be held liable. If board members knew that a dangerous situation existed in a school or program and made no attempt to develop policy to govern the situation, it is very likely that board members could be found to have violated their duties.

Proximate cause. The third requirement of negligence is that the violation of duty must be the proximate cause of an injury. The action or inaction of the person must have been a contributing factor to the injury. Simply put, if the person had acted as a reasonable person should act and if proper supervision were provided, the injury would not have occurred. The court or jury has to determine whether proper supervision could have prevented the injury and, in so deciding, the court has to look at the facts of each individual case.

The case of *Smith vs. Archbishop of St. Louis,* 632 S.W. 2d 215 (Mo. Ct. App. 1982), illustrates the concept of proximate cause. In this case, a second-grade teacher kept a lighted candle on her desk every day during the month of May. She gave no special instructions to the students regarding the danger of a lighted candle. On the morning of a school play, the plaintiff was dressed in a costume partially composed of crepe paper. While the teacher was helping students in another part of the room, the plaintiff's costume caught fire. The teacher had difficulty putting out the flames and the child sustained serious facial and upper body burns that necessitated several operations and painful treatments. The court awarded substantial damages to the child.

The *Smith* case illustrates the concept of foreseeability. The plaintiff did not have to prove that the defendant could foresee that a particular injury (child's catching fire) had to occur. The plaintiff had only to establish that a reasonable person could have foreseen that injuries could result from having an unattended lighted candle in a second-grade classroom when no safety instructions had been given to students.

In cases involving Catholic schools and programs, board members are sometimes sued both individually and in their capacities as board members. In a case such as *Smith*, the court would look for the existence of appropriate policy and of appropriate action by the person charged with the implementation of that policy—the administrator.

Negligence is a difficult concept to understand fully, and it is often difficult to predict what a court will determine to be proximate cause in any particular allegation of negligence. Spontaneous injuries that would have occurred even if a supervisor had been present may result in a court's deciding that the institution and the teacher cannot be charged with negligence. The importance of promulgating safety procedures and supervisory policies is obvious.

Injury. No matter how irresponsible the behavior of the person in authority, there is no negligence if there is no injury. If a teacher leaves 20 first graders unsupervised near a lake and no one is injured, there can be no finding of negligence and, hence, no tort. Any reasonable person, though, can see that no one in authority should routinely take risks that could result in injury.

Most negligence cases occur in classrooms because that is where students and teachers spend most of their time. However, other areas are potentially more dangerous than the classroom, and teachers and administrators will be expected to exercise a greater standard of care.

Shop, lab, and physical education classes contain great potential for injury, and cases indicate that courts expect teachers to exercise greater caution than they would in ordinary classrooms. Schools are expected to maintain equipment in working order and to keep areas free of unnecessary hazards. It is also expected that students will be given safety instructions regarding the use of potentially dangerous equipment.

Even if every possible precaution were taken, the possibility for student injury during athletics is very high. Boards and administrators, who very often are content to let athletic directors and coaches worry about athletic programs, have very real duties to ensure that competent, properly trained personnel serve as coaches for teams; that clear procedures, including documentation, are followed when accidents occur; that there is no delay in seeking medical attention when even the slightest possibility exists that medical help might be needed; and that equipment and playing areas are as hazard-free as possible.

A common legal standard judging supervision cases is: "The younger the child chronologically or mentally, the greater the standard of care expected." It might be acceptable to leave a group of high school seniors alone for ten minutes in a math class when it would not be acceptable to leave a group of first graders alone. It is reasonable to expect that 15-year-olds of average intelligence could observe traffic signals when crossing a street, but it would not be reasonable to expect mentally handicapped 15-year-olds to be responsible for crossing the street.

Board members will not, of course, be responsible for actual supervision of children and adolescents. But boards are responsible for seeing that appropriate policies and procedures for supervision are in place and are being implemented.

In developing and implementing policies for supervision, the educator and/or board member must keep in mind the reasonableness standard and ask: "Is this what one would expect a reasonable person in a similar situation to do?" No one is expected to think of every possible situation that might occur. A court would not necessarily consider it unreasonable if a school did not have a rule prohibiting throwing chairs; the court would expect, though, that there would be some sort of rule encompassing the possibility of such an activity, for example, "Students are not to throw objects." No one can foresee everything that might happen, but reasonable persons can assume that certain situations might be potentially dangerous. The teacher in the *Smith* case should have foreseen that an open flame might injure second graders.

The best defense for boards and administrators in a negligence suit is a reasonable attempt to provide for the safety of those entrusted to their care by the development and implementation of rules and policies. The reasonable board is one that ensures that administrators supervise teachers and other staff members in their implementation of rules and policies.

CORPORAL PUNISHMENT

Corporal punishment is one of the most controversial topics in education today. The laws of some states allow corporal punishment in public schools under certain conditions, but say nothing about the private school. When the first edition of *A Primer on School Law: A Guide for Board Members in Catholic Schools*[6] appeared in 1988, very few states outlawed corporal punishment; as the new millennium begins, the majority of states do.

The private school or program may not be governed by the same rules in regard to corporal punishment as is the public school. Unless corporal punishment is prohibited in all education programs by state law, Catholic schools/programs may use it. Because of growing awareness of child abuse concerns as well as psychological considerations, however, the use of corporal punishment is a legal risk. Catholic education personnel are not immune to civil tort cases or criminal charges of assault and battery if corporal punishment results in injury to the student.

With so many states and schools outlawing corporal punishment, the reader may wonder why the concept is included here. Many educators do not seem to understand exactly what corporal punishment is. Corporal punishment has been defined by many as any punitive touching. The days of swatting a student with a book or ruler are largely over, but subtler problem areas persist.

SEARCH AND SIEZURE

The 1985 case, *New Jersey v. T.L.O.*, 105 S. Ct. 733, recognized the right of public school officials to conduct searches if reasonable suspicion, rather than the stricter standard of probable cause, exists.

Catholic schools/programs, although not bound to observe even the reasonable cause standard, should, nonetheless, have some kind of policy for searching students and/or seizing their possessions. Searching a student should require "more" cause than searching a locker.

Private schools and programs could be subject to tort suits if a student alleges harm as a result of an unreasonable search. Catholic educational administrators could be charged with the torts of assault and battery and/or invasion of privacy if appropriate search and seizure procedures are not properly followed.

DEFAMATION

Defamation is the violation of a person's liberty, interest, or right to reputation. According to *Black's Law Dictionary*, defamation:

Includes both libel [what is written] and slander [what is spoken]. Defamation is that which tends to injure the reputation; to diminish the esteem, respect, goodwill or confidence in which the plaintiff is held, or to excite adverse, derogatory or unpleasant feelings or opinions against him…. A communication is defamatory if it tends so to harm the reputation of another as to lower him in the estimation of the community or to deter third persons from associating or dealing with him. (p. 375)

The potential for allegations of defamation certainly exists in Catholic schools and programs. It is important that school/program officials be factual in their comments, whether written or oral, about the conduct of students or employees. The same cautions exist whether one is dealing with students or teachers.

It is a commonly accepted rule that a person charged with defamation cannot be found guilty if what was said is true. While one neighbor sued by another for defamation could claim the affirmative defense of truth, teachers and other staff members are held to higher standards. Generally, those involved in education can use truth as a valid defense only if the statements were made without malice and to someone with a legitimate right to hear the statement. For instance, if a school board member knows that a teacher some years ago obtained an illegal abortion or completed a drug or alcohol rehabilitation program, he or she has no right to communicate that knowledge to a third party who has no legitimate reason for receiving that information.

When making statements or writing entries in records, a person should restrict statements to pertinent facts. The *Family Educational Rights and Privacy Act of 1974* changed the rules on record-keeping so that students and parents would be protected, but many schools and programs, including Catholic ones, still place potentially damaging information in school folders. Catholic education boards should ensure that there are record-keeping policies in place that: 1) limit contents of records to what is absolutely necessary; 2) provide for periodic culling of older records; and 3) limit access to records to appropriate persons, such as administrators and professional staff who have legitimate reasons for reading files.

It is generally held that teachers and other employees have legal as well as moral rights to see whatever is in their files. Only school administrators should have access to teacher files. School board members have no legal right of access to student or teacher records.

This chapter on tort liability has discussed several areas of legal concern for Catholic schools and programs and, hence, for persons serving on Catholic school boards. It is important for board members to understand that they are not responsible for deciding which actions an administrator will take, but for developing the policies that guide the administrator in making decisions.

REFLECTION QUESTIONS

1. The school principal recently announced that the school uniform for the coming academic year will be brown skirts or slacks and orange sweaters. Brown and orange are not the school colors. Many parents and students are upset and want to retain the traditional blue and white uniforms. The board has received a petition signed by more than 200 parents and students asking that the principal leave the uniforms alone. The principal says she has always liked the orange/brown combination and since uniform color is an administrative decision, the school board can have nothing to say about it. How should the board respond?

2. Are there areas of the school/parish building or administrative practices that you consider legally dangerous? Discuss ways the board can aid the administrator in addressing your concerns.

4

Duties and Rights
of Employees

DUTIES

Administrators, teachers, and other staff members are crucial in the formation and growth of the educational community. There are two broad categories of duties for administrators and staff: 1) to develop and communicate rules and policies and 2) to supervise staff members. Almost every action an administrator takes can be placed under one of these two categories.

Even though boards and pastors may have the responsibility for ultimately approving policy, the principal or other chief administrator should play a crucial role in developing it. It is hard to imagine a Catholic education board writing and approving policy without seeking the administrator's input. The best models for policy development are those which follow one of the following two procedures: 1) the administrator writes the first draft of the policy and brings it to the board or a board committee for consideration or 2) the administrator serves as a member of a committee charged with developing policy in a given area or areas. Board members should see the administrator as the educational expert and should utilize that expertise to the maximum extent possible for the good of all segments of the educational community. Administrators also communicate policy and provide for its implementation.

One of their most serious responsibilities is the supervision of teachers and staff. It is crucial that board members understand that supervision and evaluation of staff and teachers are not the board's tasks but are the responsibilities of the principal or other administrators. The principal is supposed to ensure that teaching and learning are taking place in the school. In a very real sense, supervision of teachers and other staff members is quality control.

Supervision of personnel is not simply quality control and assurance that the employee is doing a good job; it is also job protection for the employee. If a school principal, for example, does not supervise a teacher or does so carelessly, it will be very difficult for the principal to support a teacher if allegations are made that the teacher is not doing a good job. If a teacher is faced with a malpractice suit and is charged with not teaching or teaching inadequately concepts and skills that students need (such as reading), the principal is the person best equipped to assist the teacher in meeting those charges. Ideally, the supervisory data that the principal has kept will show that the teacher was teaching concepts and skills in an appropriate manner.

The duties of teachers and other supervisors can also be classified under two headings: 1) implementing rules and 2) supervising the safety and learning of students.

Teachers and other employees need to understand that their role is to implement rules, even if they do not personally agree with them. Lack of agreement is not a reason to fail to enforce a rule. If an individual cannot support a given rule or policy, that individual can use whatever channels exist to change the rule, but until a change is made by the appropriate authority, the employee is obligated to follow the rule. If a person cannot, in conscience, support the action required and change cannot be effected, then that person's only real choice is to leave the situation and seek other employment.

Teachers and staff members also are responsible for the supervision of the safety and learning of children. It is important for everyone to understand that supervision is both a mental and a physical act. It is not enough that a person is physically present; the person must be mentally present as well. If children were injured while staff members were present, a court would try to determine whether the staff members were, and/or whether they should have been, aware of the danger. For example, if two teachers were supervising recess and were conversing with each other and not aware of rock-throwing taking place in another part of the playground, a court could rule that the teachers failed to exercise mental supervision. It is simply not sufficient that teachers or other supervisors be present; those persons must be mentally present to the situation.

Nonetheless, teachers and other staff members in private institutions do have rights. The contract or agreement existing between the employee and the institution generally confers these rights. The law of contracts governs the employment situation and may govern volunteers. State statutes may confer additional rights as well. Staff members may also be said to hold rights under the common law. Although the concept of common law rights is obvious in theory, it is somewhat more difficult to delineate in legal practice. What may seem to be a principle of common law to one person may not seem so to another. One person may consider it immoral to dismiss an employee for freely speaking about administrative practices, for instance, while another may deem dismissing a person for such a reason as perfectly acceptable. Indeed, courts have upheld such dismissals.

In attempting to draw up a listing of teacher rights in Catholic schools and parishes, one could look first to the Gospel and then to common law. Appropriate questions for anyone involved in Catholic education to ask before deciding on a policy or a course of action would be: "What would Jesus do if he were in this situation? What action would be most in line with the demands of the Gospel?"

An example illustrates. Since most Catholic schools do not have a tenure system guaranteeing continuing employment, a Catholic school would be well within its rights to terminate the contract of a teacher who could no longer work because of terminal illness. The school probably has no legal responsibility to provide any financial aid to the person. But surely the Gospel demands that, in simple justice, a school do whatever it can for a person who has served it and is now in a position of need.

DISCIPLINE AND DISMISSAL

Rights

Most cases involving education in both the public and private sector are concerned with teacher dismissals and/or the nonrenewal of contracts. Obviously, a decision to dismiss or not renew the contract of an employee is one that should not be made lightly and only after other attempts at discipline of the employee have been made. When a decision is made, the administrator must proceed according to the policies in place.

Courts will scrutinize the contract to ensure that its provisions have been followed. While a private sector contract may be far less involved than a public one, it is nonetheless a contract. Courts also construe handbooks and policy statements as part of the contract existing between staff member and employer and can hold Catholic schools and parishes to the provisions of such documents.

There is a growing movement in Catholic education to abolish contracts so that both parties are free to end the relationship at any time. If such a policy is adopted, board members must carefully consider what they are doing and ensure that principles of social justice are followed.

Public school teachers may be discharged for a variety of reasons. Generally, the following are legitimate grounds for dismissal in the public sector: incompetence, insubordination, incapacity (both mental and physical), immorality (subject to community standards of what is moral), and unprofessional conduct. Catholic education board members and officials should be familiar with the laws governing dismissal in the public sector, which can serve as guidelines in developing policies and procedures in dioceses, parishes, and schools.

A quick survey of the laws of any state will reveal the problems involved in defining the causes for dismissal. What is incompetence? Who decides what it is? When is it serious enough to warrant dismissal?

Courts generally apply "the whole record test" in public sector cases except in situations such as criminal conviction or other gross misconduct. In any situation, public or private, policies should call for extensive and complete documentation of all evidence supporting a decision to dismiss or not to renew a contract.

While Catholic institutions will not be required to reinstate an employee who has been wrongfully terminated, a court can order the institution to pay the employee substantial damages. For legal as well as moral reasons, Catholic schools and programs should develop and follow sound employment policies.

Catholic education employees are bound to the terms of their contract or agreement with the institution that employs them. Violations of contract terms in Catholic schools and programs can be grounds for dismissal and courts will uphold dismissals based on such violations.

Catholic schools, with the exception of those with unions, generally do not grant tenure. Formerly, courts scrutinized the policies of institutions without formal tenure policies to see if there were policies in existence such that *de facto* tenure exists. If a Catholic school or program does not grant tenure to teachers or staff, the handbook or policy should state that there is no tenure and no expectation that employment will continue beyond a given contract year. In the last several years, there have been no significant cases of *de facto* tenure.

One situation in which public school tenured teachers can legitimately be dismissed is "reduction in force" (commonly referred to as RIF). If the student population declines or financial constraints are present, teachers may be dismissed. Today some Catholic dioceses and parishes are facing the need to reduce staff. Criteria concerning reduction in force and related policies and procedures should normally be in place before administrators make the decision to reduce staff.

Illustration in Case Law

A very significant Catholic school teacher employment case arose in New Hampshire in 1982 when four religious sisters who did not have tenure brought suit against the school superintendent, the bishop, and members of the school board because of their dismissal as principal and teachers in a Catholic school, *Reardon et al. v. LeMoyne et al.*, 454 A2d 428 (N.H. 1982). This case marked the first time a group of Catholic sisters sought legal action against church officials in a civil court. Attorneys for the diocese sought to establish that the First Amendment guarantee of the separation of church and state precluded the civil court's becoming involved in this dispute.

The superintendent notified the sisters in February that he intended not to recommend that their contracts be renewed. The superintendent so notified the parish school board which, in turn, notified the sisters that their contracts would not be renewed because of the superintendent's objections. The sisters then requested a public hearing before the school board. This request was denied on the grounds that they had no guarantee of continuing employment and, therefore, their situation was one of nonrenewal and not of termination.

The crux of the problem seemed to be the language of the

contract and handbook and the fact that the sisters signed the same yearly contract as did the lay teachers in the school. The language was, at best, ambiguous. The handbook indicated that the school would terminate the teacher's employment at the end of the school year during which the employee attainted his or her 70th birthday. (Readers should note that current law forbids the establishment of mandatory retirement age, except in certain very limited positions such as airline pilots and air traffic controllers.) The policy also stated that if a contract were not to be renewed, the party was to be notified in writing and given well-documented reasons for the nonrenewal. The contract contained a further provision that an employee faced with dismissal had a right to a hearing before the members of the parish school board; further, there was a right of appeal to the diocesan school board.

The trial court found that it could exercise jurisdiction only over the lay members of the school board and not over the superintendent, who was a member of a religious order, and the bishop because of the doctrine of separation of church and state.

On appeal, the state supreme court found that the doctrine of separation of church and state did not preclude jurisdiction in nondoctrinal contract matters. In essence, the state supreme court found that the trial court should have accepted jurisdiction over the bishop and the superintendent as well as over the school board members. Further, the state supreme court held that the trial court should have ruled on the requests made by the sisters so that their rights would have been protected.

In the end, the case was remanded to the trial court to order the school board to conduct a hearing for the sisters. Subsequently, the sisters and the other parties settled out of court; the sisters did not regain their positions.

Reardon illustrates the extreme importance of contract language. One cannot ask members of a religious congregation or anyone else to sign an employment contract and then expect not to be held to the provisions of the contract. The school board should have granted the sisters a hearing because that is what the contract said the board would do when such a hearing was requested.

Catholic administrators and boards cannot hide behind the First Amendment's protection of separation of church and state as a cover for any actions they wish to take. The courts have made it clear that they do have jurisdiction over the elements of a contract made with a religious entity, particularly over nondoctrinal issues.

While constitutional due process is not required of Catholic schools, basic fairness is. For example, a Catholic school would not have to permit a teacher facing dismissal to be represented by legal counsel at a hearing; however, there would be an expectation that the teacher would be able to hear and answer charges.

Thus, employees in Catholic institutions have rights that must be protected. Board members and administrators are responsible for knowing what those rights are and for providing protection. Written policies and guidelines greatly facilitate both the knowledge and protection of rights.

REFLECTION QUESTIONS

1. The director of religious education has just informed the board of her dilemma with regard to her secretary, a 66-year-old woman named Marge. Marge's father and grandfather were part of the group who raised money for the church when it was built 75 years ago. Marge has worked in the parish or school for the last 40 years. Marge, who has never married and has no income other than her salary, lives in a small furnished apartment. Because she is unfailingly generous and gives any excess money to charity, she has no savings and is qualified to receive only minimum social security benefits. Marge is showing increasing signs of senile dementia: forgets messages, often screams at visitors, and once shook a 5-year-old by his collar because he giggled at her unmatched socks. The DRE finds herself doing much of the clerical work and is exhausted. She needs a new secretary but she also wants to be fair to Marge. What alternatives do you see? What would you, a board member, recommend?

2. The board is considering a letter written by a teacher who has been informed that his contract will not be renewed for the coming year. The teacher demands a "full and complete trial so that the board can overturn the principal's stupid decision." How should the board respond to the letter?

5

Duties and Responsibilities of Board Members

B oard members have responsibilities for the mandates found in the board's constitution or bylaws. Generally, a board approves the budget, endorses programs, sets tuition, and establishes hiring and dismissal procedures. Another party, such as a parish council, a pastor, or an official of the religious congregation, may have final approval of all policies recommended by a board.

The board monitors the programs, the budget, and the implementation of policy. The principal, president, or other administrator who is the board's chief executive officer would certainly suggest policies and would perhaps write the first drafts of policies. The board would approve the policies (passing them to another party for final approval, as appropriate) and hold the principal accountable for their implementation. The board should, therefore, develop a plan for the evaluation of the administrator's job performance insofar as it affects the operation of the board.

DUTIES TO A DIOCESE/CHURCH

The education board has definite duties to the diocese and to the tenets of the Catholic faith. If a school is a parish school or one owned by the diocese, the board must ensure that the policies it develops are consistent with those already established by the diocese. If, for example, diocesan policy states that only Catholics who actively practice their religion in accordance with church teaching may be hired in schools owned and operated by the diocese or parishes within the diocese, the local school board must ensure that its policies are consistent with this policy of the diocese. Practically speaking, this would mean that divorced Catholics who have contracted a second marriage without an annulment are not hired or rehired. The most important factor to consider here is consistency. Many diocesan policies hold that employees do not have to be terminated solely because of conduct inconsistent with church teachings unless the conduct becomes a source of scandal. Either approach is legally defensible. Board members must realize that many injustices occur when policies and rules are applied inconsistently or when a local board attempts to act at variance with diocesan policy. These same principles should be applied in religious education and youth ministry settings.

If the board or specific members of the board cannot agree with a given diocesan policy, then change must be sought through the appropriate channels. A board is not free to adopt a policy at variance with established diocesan policy. The board's responsibility is clear: to uphold the policies of the diocese and to develop local policies in harmony with those of the diocese.

These realities are also true when a religious congregation sponsors a school or program. The board must accept rules that support the philosophy and goals of the sponsoring group. However, the relationship between such a Catholic school or program and the diocese is not always clearly defined or understood. Although social justice demands otherwise, a parish or school might be free to have a salary scale that is lower or higher than the diocesan scale. The one nonnegotiable area would be that of faith and morals. Any Catholic school or program exists under the primary authority of the bishop and so is subject to him in the area of faith and morals. As stated earlier in this text, a school or program that wishes to be truly Catholic can never be completely independent of the bishop.

Cases involving faith and morals can be very complex and emotional. For example, it can be very difficult to terminate the contract of a person who has worked in a Catholic school or program for many years because that person enters into a marriage that the church does not recognize as lawful. But if an administrator retains such an individual in contradiction to existing diocesan policy and this retention becomes the basis of scandal, the board cannot expect diocesan support. When tensions arise, board members must keep their responsibilities to the diocese and to the church in view. If a board member cannot support a policy, then the only real choice is to resign from the board.

DUTIES TO THE PRINCIPAL/ADMINISTRATOR

Since the board probably has a significant part in the selection process for the principal/administrator, its first responsibility is to ensure that the person selected meets the qualifications set by the diocese or sponsoring party.

The board also should annually review the criteria and procedures for the evaluation of the principal's job performance and ensure that the evaluation, or at least the board's part of the process, is being conducted according to policy. If evaluation is omitted or done casually, problems can result when a board later attempts to call a principal or other administrator to accountability and/or begins to consider nonrenewal of contract. It is certainly not moral, and it may well be a breach of contract, for a board to vote for nonrenewal or recommendation of non-renewal of an administrator's contract without the person's having had some evaluative feedback and an opportunity to correct any deficiencies.

Just as supervision and evaluation of staff constitute job protection for them, so evaluation of the administrator should be viewed as job protection, as well as assurance that the administrator is functioning satisfactorily in the position. If the chief administrator is found to be deficient in job performance and improvement plans are not effective, it is the board's responsibility to move into dismissal proceedings unless some other party clearly has that responsibility.

The principal or administrator has the right to expect that the administration of the school/program is his or her responsibility and that board members will not interfere in day-to-day operations. It is often easy for a board member to succumb to the temptation to become involved in disciplinary matters, academic disputes, and/or staff and administrator problems. The board member must bear in mind that board responsibilities are twofold: 1) to develop policies and 2) to support the persons and activities implementing those policies.

If the board cannot support the administrator's decisions, the board should call an executive session, one in which no one other than board members and the administrator are in attendance. In that session, board members can state their views and listen to those of the administrator. The administrator might be asked to develop different policy implementation plans. Goals and objectives are ways of implementing policies; the administrator may be able to make modifications that would be acceptable to the board. Ideally, the board and the administrator can come to some understanding and/or compromise. If no compromise can be reached that both parties can support, the board may have to call in an outside facilitator or arbitrator.

Disagreements should be left in the boardroom. Board members must constantly remember that their power functions when the board is in session; no power is vested in individual board members. Becoming involved in administrative/parent, staff/parent, or administrative/teacher disputes only weakens the authority of both the administrator and the board. The administrator, however, should keep board members informed about problems or potential problem situations so that board members will be able to respond in an intelligent manner if they are questioned.

In the end, if the board and/or the pastor or other appropriate party cannot support the administrator, the administrator will have to leave the situation. The most crucial relationship for the success of the educational ministry is that of the board and the administrator. That relationship should foster a sound academic experience in a Christian community. When the administrator and the board respect the rights of one another and promote healthy dialogue and the resolution of differences, the teaching ministry of the church should thrive.

As the board has responsibility for the evaluation of the job performance of the administrator, the administrator has responsibility for the hiring, supervision, and evaluation of teachers and/or staff. As stated in chapter 4, teacher/staff evaluation is not the board's role, but the development of personnel policies is. The board should set policies requiring regular supervision and evaluation of teachers and other staff. How the administrator implements the policies is his or her responsibility.

DUTIES TO TEACHERS/STAFF MEMBERS

Among the board's responsibilities to teachers and staff members is approval of the handbooks as policy. All schools should have faculty handbooks, and all programs should have staff handbooks. The administrator is the person who is probably best equipped to make recommendations about what should be in the handbook. This procedure protects everyone in schools or programs. It is a built-in system of checks and balances. If the administrator is very far afield, board members can tactfully suggest another approach or policy. Faculty and staff handbooks range in size from a few pages stapled together to books of 100 or more pages. The minimum matters to be included in faculty/staff handbooks are noted below. An outline of expectations regarding teaching duties, such as the construction of lesson plans, homework policies, and grading standards is needed. Nonteaching duties, generally more controversial than teaching duties, should also be addressed. Requirements such as cafeteria, playground, and study hall supervision should be discussed. The procedures governing field trips should be detailed. If an unfortunate accident were to occur on a field trip and no specific policies were in place, a teacher or other staff member could rightfully claim that the education board was at fault for failing to ensure that proper procedures be followed.

The high school has long been home to many extracurricular activities, and today more and more such activities are found in the elementary school. Student councils, drama clubs, musical productions, and athletic programs are growing in the elementary as well as the high school, and staff members must be found to moderate and coach these activities. The board must ensure that whatever is expected of teachers and/or staff in regard to extracurricular activities is stated before contracts are signed.

Job protection for teachers and staff in Catholic schools and programs is another legitimate concern. Although a 1979 case, *National Labor Relations Board v. the Catholic Bishop of Chicago, et al.*, 440 U.S. 490, rendered the creation of new unions in Catholic schools somewhat unlikely, there are unions in some Catholic school systems that existed prior to 1979. If a legitimate union exists, the board must work through it. However, most Catholic schools, particularly grade schools, are not unionized.

In the public sector, due process demands that an accused person be given notice and a hearing before an impartial tribunal. Further, the individual has the right to question accusers, provide witnesses on his or her own behalf, and to have an attorney present. The person also has the right to appeal the decision. At the minimum, Catholic education boards should develop policies requiring that an employee facing suspension or dismissal be told of the charges and be given an opportunity to refute them. Some process of appeal should be in place. In some dioceses, the bishop will be the last court of appeal; in others, the pastor has that role.

If the parish school or the diocese does not have a grievance procedure, the local education board should begin developing one to ensure that employees are treated fairly. A grievance procedure should provide a mechanism through which problems can be settled at the lowest possible level. The first step might be to discuss the problem informally with the administrator. Then a written document could be submitted. A third step could be a committee of the board. Finally, the whole board could consider the grievance. What constitutes matter for a grievance should be clearly stated. Every disagreement an employee has with a principal is not a potential grievance. Only serious situations that cannot be solved through other channels should be brought to a grievance procedure.

DUTIES TO PARENT/STUDENT COMMUNITY

A fourth group to which the board has specific responsibilities is the parent/student community. All schools and programs should have a parent/student handbook in which the policies that affect these persons are explained. Some areas to be included are: admission policies, academic policies, the procedure for communication between parents and teachers and/or administration, the discipline code, rules concerning activities, field trip policies and forms, emergency procedures, parent service and fund-raising requirements, and the role of the education board.

Parents should be informed about the function of the education board and about the policies governing attendance at board meetings, speaking at board meetings, and bringing matters to the attention of the board. Boards must guard against becoming a "dumping ground" for complaints. Only serious matters that appropriately belong before the school board should be considered and then only after all other channels have been exhausted. Boards should not become involved in matters that are the province of principals, other administrators, and staff members.

Board members have serious responsibilities to the church, to the diocese, to the parish or parishes that sponsor the school or program, to the sponsoring religious congregation, to the administrator, to teachers and staff, and to parents and students. The role of the board member is to oversee the operation of solid education and effective ministry through the development of sound policy.

As discussed earlier, most boards are consultative and members face little legal liability in most instances. However, as a matter of simple justice, parishes and schools should provide liability insurance for board members. The National Association of Boards of Catholic Education of the National Catholic Educational Association may be contacted for information regarding liability insurance.

REFLECTION QUESTIONS

1. Assume that your school or program has no faculty/staff handbook. The administrator has asked the board for some help in initiating the handbook process. What elements would you identify as belonging in such a handbook? How might the administrator begin the process?

2. The school principal has brought the board a dilemma. She has heard increasing rumors that one of the female teachers is lesbian and is planning a commitment ceremony with her intended partner. Today another teacher showed the principal an invitation to the wedding. The principal tells the board that she makes it a policy never to check on people's private behavior. Nevertheless, she has told all staff members that if their behavior causes a scandal, they will be dismissed. What would you advise the principal to do?

The first five chapters of this text are intended to present an overview of the laws affecting Catholic education and board members. Each remaining chapter will discuss a special topic area followed by reflection questions.

6

Privacy and Reputation

P rivacy and reputation are two serious legal issues facing Catholic educators today. Both students and staff members expect that information concerning them will be revealed only to those with a right to know. Board members must ensure that policies requiring the use of reasonable measures to safeguard such information are in place. To do otherwise could mean that the school or parish could face civil lawsuits for defamation of character.

DEFAMATION OF CHARACTER

As stated in the previous chapter, defamation is an unprivileged communication that harms the reputation of another. Defamation, which may involve invasion of privacy, can be either spoken, (slander), or written, (libel).

All members of the education community should be concerned with protecting the reputations of all in their schools and programs. Educators should exercise great care in keeping student records, as well as in speaking about students and behavior. It is only just that parish, program administrators, and board members should refrain from gossip or unnecessary derogatory remarks about staff and/or students. The best advice for everyone is to be as factual as possible in official documents and to refrain from "editorial" comments. Whatever is written should meet the following three criteria: it should be specific, it should be behaviorally oriented, and it should be verifiable.

Board members should review policies posing potential privacy and reputation problems. Such policies should be as clear as possible and leave little room for doubt. It is more professional, and legally more appropriate, to write, "Bob has been absent four times this month, late for class eight times, and sent to the assistant principal's office for disrupting class three times," than to write "Bobby is absent too much, late most of the time, and always in trouble." It is better to write, "Susan is reading on a first-grade level" than to write, "Susan can't read."

Student files present special problems. Past practices often included using student folders as a collection place for any and all items. It was, and in some cases still is, the norm to find absentee notes, student papers, old non-standardized tests, and the like in a student's file. The best approach to file safety is to limit the contents of official files to the following: academic transcripts, standardized test results, health form(s), and emergency sheets. Everything else can and should be stored elsewhere. If there is no reason to have an item in a student's file, it should be stored elsewhere. Disciplinary records, in particular, should not be stored in official files. Students are still in a formative stage, and officials should exercise extreme caution in storing information that could be harmful to a student. Disciplinary records should not be a part of the information sent to another institution when a student transfers or graduates. If the new school requires disciplinary information, the transferring school should consider preparing a document containing the information and having the parents sign a statement that they have seen the document and agree to its being sent.

In today's litigious society, most administrators are familiar with the problems of writing legally non-controversial recommendations without sacrificing the truth. Further, most people have read recommendations that seem to say very little. Although educators must understand that no one has an absolute, legal right to a recommendation, fairness would indicate that only the most extreme situations should result in a student being denied a recommendation. College recommendations pose particular problems. For example, a student or parent may demand a recommendation from a certain teacher if the recommendation must come from a teacher in a given discipline. If a teacher were to decline to write the recommendation, the parent would probably complain to the principal and/or guidance department head and the teacher may become embroiled in a dispute in which there are no winners.

Students can receive letters verifying enrollment, and factual statements can be made about education and participation in extra-curricular activities. The guideline is to be as fair as possible. School and program officials should strive to be just and respectful of the dignity of others in all communications, whether official or not, and to say only what can be shown to have some valid relationship to the professional situation. In so doing, school officials protect them-selves against possible lawsuits alleging defamation and/or invasion of privacy.

CONFIDENTIALITY OF RECORDS

An issue related to invasion of privacy is confidentiality of records. If administrators follow the procedures outlined above, the risk of having problematic materials in student files becomes minimal.

The contents of student files should be released only to autho-rized persons. Even faculty and staff members should have access to student files only for appropriate, education-related reasons. Paren-tal signatures should be required before records are sent to anyone. Board members have no right of access to student files and should view students' records only when considering a grievance.

Many persons associated with Catholic schools can recall when neither they nor students' parents were permitted access to student records. Then, in 1975, Congress passed the Buckley Amendment, granting students and parents the right to inspect school records. Some legal experts believe that the Buckley Amendment does not apply to private schools. The amendment contains a clause stating that the legislation does not apply to private schools *solely* because of the presence of government funds (e.g., federal commodities in cafeterias, bloc grant money). However, this belief has never been tested in court.

In some cases private sector officials have been required to comply with federal legislation, such as antidiscrimination statutes. The requirement was based on public policy considerations and commonly accepted standards of behavior. It is better to comply *voluntarily* with legislation such as the Buckley Amendment than to risk becoming a test case for the courts. Legalities aside, it seems only right that persons affected by records have the right to see them.

REFLECTION QUESTION

1. A group of parents "corner" a group of board members at a student activity. The parents are concerned about the recommendations teachers are writing for their children. The parents maintain that the teachers are writing the bare minimum and are not saying the sorts of things needed to guarantee acceptance at some of the "better" schools. What will you say?

7

Staff and Student Relationships

Teachers and other staff members care about young people, and that concern extends to all areas of student life. Educators often find themselves counseling students in personal matters. It is not unusual for a teacher, catechist, or youth minister to find him/herself in the position of "surrogate parent," and students often entrust these adults with confidential information. Since many have little training in professional counseling, teachers and staff members often question what is appropriate in interacting with students outside the classroom setting.

Few guidelines are available. Teachers and other personnel often deal with situations that pose personal and legal risks for themselves as well as for the students. This author is familiar with several situations in which parents threatened and/or pursued legal action against a teacher whose actions they viewed as unwise, inappropriate, sexually motivated, or interfering with the parent/child relationship. All adults working in the educational ministry of the church should be aware of the legal ramifications involved in student/staff relationships, and be careful to avoid the perception as well as the reality of inappropriateness. Board members should exercise diligence in reviewing pertinent policies, particularly those in faculty and/or staff handbooks, and administrators must be alert for any potentially problematic situations.

CONFIDENTIALITY

Most educators rightfully consider student confidences sacred. If a student confides in a teacher, the student should be able to presume that the confidential information normally will not be shared with anyone. Educators may believe that they have some type of immunity that protects them from legal liability if they refuse to share student information given in confidence.

However, the facts indicate that very few states provide any sort of immunity or privilege for teachers who receive confidential information from students. If a teacher or other supervising adult were subpoenaed, placed on the stand, and asked for confidential information, most judges would require the person to answer. The adult staff member does not enjoy the type of privilege that lawyers and priests have. In fact, recent case law indicates that teachers who are told in confidence by a student that he or she is going to commit suicide can be held liable for negligent homicide if the teacher says nothing and the student commits suicide.

SEXUAL MISCONDUCT

One end of the student/staff relationship spectrum is represented by sexual misconduct. Sexual misconduct can be alleged in apparently innocent situations. Students can misinterpret touching, and an educator could find him/herself facing child abuse charges. Extreme caution is in order whenever an adult touches a student.

Another kind of problem is posed by a student who believes that a teacher or supervising adult has not responded to efforts to achieve a closer relationship. Such a student may accuse an educator of inappropriate conduct as a retaliatory measure. Educators and board members must be aware that serious consequences can result from an allegation of child abuse, even if that allegation is eventually proved false. At the very least, such a false allegation is extremely embarrassing for the teacher. If a child abuse report is made, authorities will question the educator and the investigation will be recorded. Some states keep lists of suspected child abusers. Catholic education boards need to dialogue with administrators to determine the best possible policies. Virtually every diocese and archdiocese in the United States has child and sexual abuse policies. The board should officially accept the diocesan policy as the parish's and/or school's policy.

Thus, it is imperative that educators protect themselves and the students they teach by practicing appropriate behavior with students. To avoid even the slightest hint of impropriety, an adult should avoid being alone with a single student behind closed doors unless a window or other opening permits outsiders to see into the area. A good question to ask oneself might be: If this were my child, would I have any objection to a teacher's relating with him or her in this manner?

Fear of teachers facing child abuse allegations has caused some public school districts in this country to adopt rules that prohibit any faculty touching of students. Such rules preclude putting one's arm around students, patting a student on the back, and giving a student a hug. No educator would want to adopt such a position, but common sense precautions must be taken for the protection of all.

OTHER PHYSICAL CONTACT

Educators can also be charged with child abuse that is not sexual. Corporal punishment, prohibited by regulation in most Catholic schools and programs, can set the stage for allegations of physical abuse. Some parents have reported teachers for child abuse after the teacher placed a hand on a child's shoulder to bring the child to attention. Although these cases are outrageous, they do indicate the dangers that can exist. Thus, as stated earlier, educators are well advised to adopt the operating rule: Never touch a child in a way that can be construed as punitive.

OTHER BEHAVIORS

Teachers and other staff members must bear in mind that they are professionals rendering a service. Just as a counselor or psychiatrist is professionally bound to avoid emotional involvement with a client, an educator/minister should avoid becoming so emotionally involved with a young person that objectivity and fairness are compromised. Educators must remember that they have many students for whom they are responsible and who need and may desire the teacher's attention. If a relationship with a student keeps an educator from responding to other students' needs on a regular basis, the educator and his or her supervisor should seriously examine the appropriateness of the relationship.

In seeking to assess the appropriateness of an adult/student relationship, some mental health professionals recommend asking oneself questions such as these: Whose needs are being met? Is there a boundary? Where is it?

The following adult behaviors could be considered inappropriate, depending on the totality of the circumstances: dropping by a student's home, particularly if no parent is present; frequent telephoning of the student; social trips with a student; and sharing of the teacher's personal problems.

Serving as a Catholic educator in these times is a privilege and a gift. It is indeed sad when an educator is forced to relinquish that gift because of inappropriate choices. Reflection and prudent behavior will keep educators and board members legally protected and professionally fulfilled.

REFLECTION QUESTIONS

1. The school principal has asked the board to help her develop some type of policies and/or guidelines to govern student/staff relationships. How would your respond?

2. Assume for the sake of argument that no diocesan sexual abuse policy exists, and the board is charged with developing one. Discuss the elements that should be included.

8

Keeping Student Confidences

One of the more perplexing situations facing Catholic education today is presented by students' sharing confidential information. Today's young persons may well face more pressures and problems than young people of any other decade. Board members may have heard stories about teachers who failed to report student threats against self and/or others and in which the student subsequently acted on the threat. The responsibility for receiving student confidences and advising students in both day-to-day situations and crises can be overwhelming. Busy educators may well ask: "What am I supposed to do? I know I'm not a professional counselor, a psychiatrist, or a social worker, but I'm the one the student trusts, the one the student has consulted. Are there certain legal issues involved in the receiving of student confidences? Is there matter that must be made known to others, even when the student has asked for and received a promise of confidentiality from me?"

These are good questions to ask. Staff members cannot afford to think that they can help all students all the time, for such is not possible. If a student were to come to a teacher or catechist and say that he or she is experiencing shortness of breath and chest pain, the adult would quickly summon both the student's parents and medical assistance. Psychological problems are no less serious than physical ones, and the "layperson" who attempts to deal with such problems unaided may well be courting tragedy for both self and student. This chapter will address topics that should be of interest to board members: confidentiality, legal immunity of counselors, journal writing, and special situations such as retreats.

CONFIDENTIALITY

Confidentiality is generally held to mean that one individual or several individuals will keep private information that has been given to them and will not reveal it. For example, the person who receives the sacrament of reconciliation rightfully expects that the subject matter of confession will be held sacred by the confessor and will not be revealed to anyone. Indeed, there are accounts of priests who died rather than break the seal of confession.

Friends share confidences with each other. One individual may say to another, "This is confidential; you cannot repeat it." The person speaking in confidence has a right to expect that the confidant to whom the information has been given will keep the matter secret. But there are recognized limits to what friends will keep private. If one's friend confides that she has been stockpiling sleeping medication and plans to take all of it that evening so as to commit suicide, morality seems to demand that the confidant communicate that knowledge to a spouse or other family member of the confiding individual, or take some other action to intervene in the attempted suicide.

It is not unheard of for an adult who would not hesitate to get help for a friend to believe that a student who is talking about suicide is not serious, or can be talked out of the planned action, or is not capable of carrying out a threatened suicide. As child and adolescent psychologists report, young people often do not think through the long-term ramifications of suicide attempts. Also, some young people are fascinated with death, as can be seen by the idolization of famous people who have died young or committed suicide.

If a student tells a teacher, catechist, or youth minister that he or she is going to harm self or others, the adult must reveal that information, even if a promise of confidentiality has been given. In a number of lawsuits brought against teachers and school districts, parents sought damages from teachers who were told by students in confidence that they planned to harm themselves or others, but who did not contact parents or other authorities. In some cases, the educators were brought to trial on a claim of negligence by failure to warn. School shootings and related violence have resulted in a flurry of litigation. In Paducah, Kentucky, parents of the Heath High School victims have brought suit against the school district, the school, the administrators, and the teachers, alleging that the journals and writings of the perpetrator contained warning signals that the school staff disregarded. The litigation may continue for years and, regardless of which side "wins," the case fallout will be enormous in terms of student and community trust. Such cases also cause teachers to question the wisdom of journal writing and, indeed, any writing that may involve personal thoughts and feelings.

LEGAL IMMUNITY

A widely held myth purports that counselors, physicians, psychologists, and social workers have legal immunity from responsibility for any injuries that may arise from failing to act on confidential information presented to them. However, most states have abolished counselor immunity, and the few who still "have it on the books" have imposed several limitations on the concept. A counselor who hears from a young person that the individual plans to kill his or her parents and does nothing about it will not be legally able to decline to answer questions under oath, nor will the counselor be held harmless for any resulting injuries if he or she decides not to reveal the threats. Counselors, teachers, and other ministers must make it very clear to a confiding individual that they will keep confidences unless the individual's health, life, or safety or those of another are threatened. Board members, in consultation with the administrator, should seriously consider the development of a policy that directs adult staff members to tell students at the outset: "I will keep your confidences so long as no one's life, health, or safety is involved. Once life, health, or safety is involved, I cannot promise confidentiality." The only two privileges from disclosure of confidential information which seem to remain in state law are that of priest/penitent and attorney/client. Even the husband/wife privilege that allowed a spouse to refuse to testify against a spouse has been largely abandoned.

In light of the above, board members must presume that no legal protection exists for those who receive student confidences. What can board members expect of the teacher or staff member who wants to be a role model for young persons, who wants to be approachable and helpful? The answer is simple: Lay down the ground rules for confidentiality before receiving any confidences. If a student asks to talk to an adult in confidence, the adult should reiterate the ground rules before the student begins to share.

JOURNAL WRITING

In religion, language arts, English, and other subjects, teachers have long recognized the value of student journal writing. This practice does, however, carry a real risk of student disclosure of information that the adult supervisor is compelled to reveal. Teachers and other supervising adults must set the same rules for confidentiality as discussed above.

Teachers, catechists, and youth ministers must understand that they are expected to read what students write. If a person cannot read the assignment, then the assignment should not be given. In particular, staff members should avoid such techniques as telling students to clip together pages they do not wish the adult to read or to write at the top of such pages, "Please do not read." Journal writing has a place in today's educational communities, but adults must be sure that students understand the parameters of the assignment and of the adult's responsibilities for reporting threatened danger. Board members and administrators should discuss the concept of journaling and develop policies and procedures to ensure that journals are used appropriately.

RETREATS

As board members should realize, the retreat experience is extremely important for today's Catholic young people. Students are often at their most vulnerable in such situations. They may share stories of child abuse, sexual harassment, family dysfunction, even possible criminal activity. While encouraging students to share, the group leader must once again set the ground rules before the sharing beings. The use of peer leaders does not lessen the responsibility of the supervising adults. Student leaders must be told the ground rules and the necessity to communicate them to group members, as well as procedures to be followed in notifying adults if matter is revealed that must be reported.

CASE LAW

In the case *Brooks v. Logan and Joint District No. 2*, 903 P.2d 73 (1995), parents of a student who had committed suicide filed an action for wrongful death and a claim for negligent infliction of emotional distress against a teacher who had assigned the keeping of journals to her class. Jeff Brooks was a student at Meridian High School and was assigned to Ms. Logan's English class. Students were asked to make entries into a daily journal as part of their English composition work. For a period of four months prior to his death, Jeff wrote in his journal.

After his death, Ms. Logan read through the entries and gave the journal to a school counselor, who delivered it to Jeff's parents. Jeff had made journal entries that indicated that he was depressed and that he was contemplating suicide. One entry read as follows:

> Well, Edgar Allen Poe [sic], I can live with studying about that stuff he wrote especially the one short story about the evil eye.... I used to write poems until I pronounced myself dead in one of them and how could I write poems or stories if I was dead.... Recently...see I went into a medium depression and wrote poems to two special people.... I told them it was too bad that I had to say goodby this way like that but, it would be the only way and I felt better.... (p. 81)

Ms. Logan maintained that Jeff had requested that she not read his entries, so that he would feel free to express himself. The journal contained a note in which Ms. Logan stated that she would not read the journal for content, but would only check for dates and length. The parents maintained that, in a conversation with Ms. Logan after their receipt of the journal, she stated that she had "reread the entries." Ms. Logan denied that she made that statement, and contends that she did not read the entries in question until after Jeff's death.

The lower court granted summary judgment in favor of the teacher and the school district. However, the appellate court reversed the finding, and held that there were issues of fact in existence, which could only be determined at trial. Thus, a trial court was directed to determine whether Ms. Logan's actions or inactions constituted negligence contributing to Jeff's death. The court was directed to make a determination as to whether Jeff's suicide was foreseeable: Would a reasonable person in Ms. Logan's place have recognized the possibility of suicide and notified someone? The appellate court refers to similar case law in which jailers have been held liable for the suicide of prisoners when the prisoners had exhibited warning signs.

This case and the discussion indicate the vulnerability of teachers and other ministers who receive student confidences. Board members should discuss the topic of confidentiality with the school and/ or program administrator and adopt policies that will support a legally sound approach to confidentiality. The wise Catholic educator will establish and enforce ground rules for dealing with student confidences and will seek help from school officials and/or parents when appropriate.

REFLECTION QUESTIONS
1. Do board members know the parish or school rules concerning keeping student confidences? If a parent asked you, a board member, to explain those rules, how would your respond?
2. You are the board chair, and the DRE asked your advice concerning the following situation. Some students drank alcohol while on an overnight retreat. The DRE asks the board to consider a policy that would bar all overnight activities. How would you respond?

9

Child Abuse

One of the most serious issues confronting those involved in the ministry of Catholic education today is child abuse. The media carry daily reports of adults causing children physical and emotional pain. The educator is in a particularly sensitive position. Students often choose teachers or other ministers as confidants in their struggles to deal with abuse and its effects. For this reason, boards of education and principals must ensure that teachers and all other employees are as prepared as possible to deal with the realities of abuse and neglect. The board should consider adopting a policy such as: "This school or program abides by the child abuse reporting statutes of the state."

Further, policy should require that principals and other administrators spend some time reviewing pertinent state law and school/program policies and providing information and discussion on the topic at one of the first faculty meetings of the year. If a separate meeting is not provided for other employees, such as secretaries, custodians, and cafeteria workers, the board and the administrator should consider having them present for the appropriate portion of the faculty or staff meeting.

STATUTORY CONSIDERATIONS

All 50 states have laws requiring educators to report suspected abuse and/or neglect. While the actual wording varies from state to state, the statute will ordinarily require that persons who supervise children or adolescents report suspected child abuse. Some states are now requiring anyone with knowledge of possible abuse to report it. Compliance with these statutes may not be as easy as it first appears, since what arouses suspicion in one adult may not in another. Some statutes mention "reasonable suspicion." These standards could result in two teachers viewing the same situation and reaching two completely different conclusions. In such cases, courts have to determine whether each individual sincerely believed in the correctness of his or her perception.

Despite the best of intentions and efforts, teachers and other staff members may fail to report suspected child abuse. In that case, the administrator can be held liable for failure to report under the doctrine of *respondeat superior*, "let the superior answer." However, if the administrator can demonstrate that the board has an appropriate policy in place and the administrator has appropriately implemented it, responsibility for failure to report should be that of the individual staff member who failed, not of the institution.

Statutes generally mandate reporting procedures. The reporting individual usually makes a phone report that is followed by a written report within a specified time period, often 48 hours, although some states do have different procedures.

Statutes usually provide protection for a person who makes a good-faith report of child abuse which later is discovered to be unfounded. Such a good-faith reporter will not be liable to the alleged abuser for defamation of character. However, a person can be held liable for making what is referred to as a "malicious report," one which has no basis in fact and which was made by a person who knows that no factual basis existed. Conversely, statutes usually mandate that a person who knew of child abuse or neglect and failed to report it can be fined and/or charged with a misdemeanor or felony.

DEFINING AND REPORTING ABUSE

What is child abuse? This author once heard another attorney define it as "corporal punishment gone too far." Although it excludes sexual abuse, the definition has merit. However, it poses questions: How far is too far? Who makes the final determination? Can what one person considers abuse be considered valid corporal punishment by another? Are there any allowances for differing cultural practices?

It is difficult, if not impossible, to give a precise definition that will cover all eventualities. Certainly, some situations are so extreme that there can be little argument that abuse has occurred. Someone *has* abused a student who appears at school with cigarette burns.

However, when a child alleges sexual abuse, the investigating agency will have to determine whether the child is telling the truth, lying, or somehow mistaken.

The majority of cases probably will not be clear-cut, and an educator may well struggle to decide if a report should be made. Many law enforcement officials and some attorneys instruct educators to report everything that students tell them that could possibly constitute abuse or negligence. They further caution teachers and other adults that it is not their job to determine if abuse has occurred. As a mandated reporter, the teacher or minister has the responsibility to present the information to the agency designated to receive reports. Appropriate officials will determine whether the report should be investigated further or simply "screened out" as a well-intentioned report that does not appear to be in the category of abuse.

Administrators should provide professional staff, other employees, and volunteers with some inservice training concerning the indicators of child abuse and neglect, and the legal procedures for reporting such conditions. Many excellent written resources are available, and local police departments and social service agencies are usually happy to provide both materials and speakers to schools and programs. If an institution does not provide its staff members with education and materials on this topic, a phone call to appropriate sources should produce the needed materials.

Many experts advise that the school administrator, usually the principal, make all child abuse and/or neglect reports, so that the same person is reporting all situations in a given school. However, individual state laws vary on this point. Some states clearly require the person with the suspicion to file the report, thus the staff member or educator must personally report abuse to the appropriate agency and notify the principal or other administrator. The last point is crucial for it is legally dangerous for the institution when a police officer or other official appears to investigate a report of child abuse and the administrator does not know that a report has been filed. Administrators should decide in advance how visits and requests from police or social workers will be handled.

Many states require that school personnel allow officials to examine and question students. Board members and administrators should seek legal counsel in determining the applicable law for a given state. If the law permits police and social workers to examine and question children, a school official should always ask to be present. In some jurisdictions, the investigating official may refuse to allow school personnel to be present.

ABUSE BY EDUCATORS/MINISTERS

A survey of educational cases decided in courts of record reveals that the number of lawsuits alleging abuse of children by teachers or other staff members is increasing. While administrators can be found responsible for the acts of subordinates, courts appear unwilling to hold administrators liable unless there is clear evidence of administrative misconduct. In the 1990 case *Medlin v. Bass*, 398 S.E.2d 460, school officials were found innocent of misconduct in their supervision of an educator guilty of abuse. The plaintiff alleged that the school was responsible for the staff member's actions under the doctrine, cited above, *respondeat superior*. However, the abuser's crime was outside the scope of employment and there existed no compelling reasons for his superiors to investigate his background more thoroughly than they did. In the 1990 case *D.T. et al. v. Ind. School District No. 16 of Pawnee City*, 894 F2d 1 176 (1980), the court declined to hold school officials responsible for teacher abuse of students occurring during summer fundraising. A particularly troubling aspect of this case was the fact that the teacher had a previous conviction for sodomy. The decision notwithstanding, it is possible that, in situations in which an employee or volunteer has a criminal record involving child abuse, other courts may find administrators guilty of negligence if they failed to take reasonable steps to check references.

It is a well-established reality that schools and churches can attract persons with abusive tendencies who are seeking children upon whom to prey. Thus, officials must do everything in their power to investigate the background of persons before employment.

Some states now mandate that persons who work with children be fingerprinted and sign an authorization of a police check of his or her name for any criminal arrests and/or convictions. Prior conviction of a crime is not an automatic, permanent bar to employment, but many states bar persons who have been convicted of a violent crime in the 10 years immediately preceding employment.

Administrators may wish to include a statement such as the following on applications: "Conviction of a crime is not an automatic bar to employment. Please give all pertinent details. Decisions will be made as required by law." This procedure can be adapted for use with volunteers.

Any student or parent complaint alleging child abuse by a teacher or other staff member must receive serious attention. Failure to do so can put the institution and its officials at grave legal risk. Administrators and school boards should adopt policies governing reporting child abuse/neglect by staff *before* the need for such policies surfaces. It is preferable to have a policy that is never needed than to have no policy and be forced to try to construct one when faced with a need.

REFLECTION QUESTIONS
1. How would you define child abuse?
2. Your daughter Melissa tells you the following story. Student Z told Melissa that she has been tied to a chair in a dark, unheated closet while her father pours water from a pitcher on her head. She is left there in freezing weather. Student Z already told one teacher about the situation, and the teacher told her to stop making up stories. She asked Melissa to ask you to turn her father into the authorities so that he will get off her back. What will you do?

10

Sexual Harassment

Given the newspaper stories of alleged sexual harassment and resulting lawsuits, board members probably have heard much about the subject. No longer is sexual harassment something that is found only between two adults or between an adult and a child. School children claim that peers have harassed them. The news stories can seem overwhelming, and the potential for legal liability great. What, then, can boards do?

Board members should enact policies that define sexual harassment, using federal and state law to assist with the process. Every comment made concerning gender is *not* sexual harassment. For example, a male student who states, "Everyone knows boys are better at math than girls," or a teacher who declares, "I'd rather teach girls since they are not as rowdy as boys," is not guilty of sexual harassment, although they may be guilty of a new tort recognized in some states as gender harassment. Title VII of the *Civil Rights Act of 1964* mandated that the workplace be free of harassment based on sex. Title IX requires that educational programs receiving federal funding be free of sexual harassment. Both these titled laws are antidiscrimination statutes.

Federal antidiscrimination law can bind Catholic institutions. Most schools and parishes routinely file statements of compliance with discrimination laws with appropriate local, state, and national authorities. Antidiscrimination legislation can impact Catholic institutions because the government has a compelling interest in the equal treatment of all citizens. Compliance with statutory law can be required if there is no less burdensome way to meet the requirements of the law.

The Equal Employment Opportunity Commission has issued guidelines that define sexual harassment, forbidden by Title VII, as:

Unwelcome sexual advances, requests for sexual favors, and other verbal or physical conduct of a sexual nature when:
- Submission to such conduct by an individual is made explicitly or implicitly a term of employment;
- Submission to, or rejection of such conduct by an individual is used as the basis for an employment decision;
- And such conduct has the purpose or effect to interfere with an individual's work performance, or creates a hostile or intimidating environment.

Although the above definition concerns employment conditions, "education" can be substituted for "employment" in the definition, and the basis for Title IX violations would be evident. Specifically, Title IX states: "No person in the United States shall, on the basis of sex, be excluded from participation in, be denied the benefits of, or be subjected to discrimination under any education program or activity receiving federal financial assistance." While the amount of financial assistance necessary to trigger protection has not been established, most Catholic schools have accepted some government funds or services at some time and thus would be well-advised to comply with Title IX as far as possible. Courts, including the U.S. Supreme Court, are vigorously supporting persons' rights to be free from sexual harassment.

In the 1992 case of *Franklin v. Gwinnet County Public Schools,* 112 S.Ct. 1028, the U.S. Supreme Court ruled that monetary damages can be awarded students whose rights under Title IX have been violated. In this case a teacher allegedly had sexually harassed a student for several years. The harassment consisted of conversations, kissing, telephone calls, and forced sexual relations. The school system maintained that no relief could be given the student since Title IX remedies had been limited to back pay and employment relief. The court disagreed, held that students who suffer harassment are entitled to damages, and remanded the case to the lower court for a determination of damages. Thus, it would appear that if Title IX applies to the Catholic school or institution (and no case to date has held that it does not), students are protected against sexual harassment in much the same manner that employees are protected.

ACTIONS THAT CAN BE HARASSMENT

Behaviors that could constitute sexual harassment include sexual propositions, off-color jokes, inappropriate physical contact, innuendoes, sexual offers, looks, and gestures. In a number of recent public school cases and in one religious education case, female students alleged that male students made sexual statements to them and that school officials, after being informed, declined to take action, stating that "boys will be boys." Many of these cases have been settled out of court and money has been paid to the alleged victims.

Although one can argue that the person who sexually harasses another should be liable and not the school or program or administrators, case law is suggesting that administrators who ignore such behavior or do not take it seriously can be held liable to the offended parties. See the 1990 case *Jane Doe v. Special School District of St. Louis County,* 901 F2d 642 (8th Cir.).

SUGGESTED POLICIES

One of the most important actions board members can take with regard to sexual harassment is to develop clear policies defining sexual harassment and detailing procedures for dealing with claims that sexual harassment has occurred. Teachers and other staff members are required to implement the policies. Following is one suggestion of a policy statement based on federal law.

Definition. Sexual harassment is defined as 1) threatening to impose adverse employment, academic, disciplinary, or other sanctions on a person unless favors are given; and/or 2) conduct containing sexual matter or suggestions which would be offensive to a reasonable person.

Sexual harassment includes, but is not limited to, the following behaviors:

1) Verbal conduct such as epithets, derogatory jokes or comments, slurs or unwanted sexual advances, imitations, or comments;

2) Visual contact such as derogatory and/or sexually oriented posters, photography, cartoons, drawings, or gestures;

3) Physical contact such as assault, unwanted touching, block-ing normal movements, or interfering with work, study, or play because of sex;

4) Threats and demands to submit to sexual requests as a condition of continued employment, grades or other ben-efits, or to avoid some other loss and offers of benefits in return for sexual favors;

5) Retaliation for having reported or threatened to report sexual harassment.

Procedures for reporting should then be given. These procedures should include a statement such as: "All allegations will be taken seriously and promptly investigated." Administrators should stress confidentiality and express concern for both the alleged victim and the alleged perpetrator. Procedures should include copies of the forms used in reporting such cases.

Every employee and volunteer should be required to sign a statement that he or she has been given a copy of the policies relating to sexual harassment and other sexual misconduct, has read the material, and agrees to be bound by it. Parent/student handbooks should contain at least a general statement that sexual harassment is not condoned in a Christian atmosphere, and both parents and students should sign a statement that they agree to be governed by the handbook.

PREVENTION

It is far easier to prevent claims of sexual harassment than it is to defend them. To that end, teachers, ministers, and volunteers should participate in some kind of inservice training that raises awareness of sexual harassment and other gender issues. Staff mem-bers must understand what sorts of behaviors can be construed as sexual harassment.

Teachers and ministers should discuss issues of fair treatment of others with their students and should promptly correct students who demean others. Defenses such as, "I was only kidding," will not be accepted if the alleged victim states that the behavior was offensive and unwelcome, and a court finds that a reasonable person could find the behavior offensive and unwelcome.

Finally, of course, sexual harassment and other forms of demeaning behavior have no place in Catholic parishes and schools. Guarding the dignity of each member of the school community should be a priority for all Catholic educators/ministers.

REFLECTION QUESTIONS
1. How would you define sexual harassment if asked to do so by a parent or student?
2. How would you handle the following scenario? You, a board member, have volunteered to supervise a student mixer. While making "rounds," you see a 13-year-old girl sitting by the bathroom and weeping. You ask what is wrong. She gives you the name of a male student and says, "He told me my cup size has to be bigger than my head. I'm afraid to go back on the dance floor. Am I really so big?"

11

Students with
Special Needs

The last several years have seen a sharp increase in litigation against Catholic schools because students with special needs are seeking admission and/or retention. A number of attempted lawsuits have been brought against parishes for failing to provide any programs for persons with special needs or for providing only seriously inadequate programs. Although it may seem that only schools should be concerned about this issue, the Gospel demands that all give at least as much attention to such persons as does the law.

Section 504 of the *Rehabilitation Act of 1973* and the *1992 Americans with Disabilities Act* can seem to be legal quagmires for the board member. Myths and half-truths abound. Some consultants and lawyers advise that schools and church buildings must be made totally accessible. Many board members and administrators fear that the cost of accommodations will be so high as to force schools and parish programs out of existence. Some school and program administrators question accepting students with special needs. Can the average Catholic school or parish provide the proper program adjustments needed by these students? Board members, as well as Catholic school and program personnel, need a clear understanding of legal requirements.

DISCRIMINATION LAW

Federal law prohibits discrimination on the basis of race, sex, disability, age, and national origin. Although discrimination on the basis of religion or creed is also prohibited, the right of religious institutions to give preference to their own members is upheld.

Practically, this means that Catholic schools and programs may give preference to Catholic students and may give hiring preference to Catholic teachers and other employees.

EDUCATION ACCESS LAWS

Board members and administrators must understand the law governing students with special needs in schools. *Public Law 94-142*, the *Education of All Handicapped Children Act*, and its successor law, the *Individuals with Disabilities in Education Act*, ensure a "free and appropriate education" for all children. There is no requirement that Catholic schools provide the "free and appropriate education." However, in situations in which the only school for the handicapped/disabled is one operated by the Catholic Church or some other private organization, the state may place a child in a private school if that placement seems to provide the most appropriate education. In such a case, the state would be responsible for the tuition.

Catholic schools and programs are not required to meet every need of every child. Most private schools are not equipped to offer all educational services to everyone. The fact that a school or program does not have to offer services does not mean that a student attending that school has no right to such services. *Public Law 94-142* and the *Individuals with Disabilities in Education Act* give students rights, and a private school student has a right to request and receive an evaluation and, if necessary, be given an Individual Educational Plan (IEP). The public school must make every reasonable effort to provide the student with services needed, even if the student remains in the private school. If it is not practical to offer such services to a private school student, the public school officials can draw up an IEP that calls for public school education. A parent is always free to accept or reject such an IEP. If a parent elects to keep a child in a private school over the objections of the professional educators working with that child, the public school cannot be held responsible for the child's progress, nor can the public school be required to pay private school tuition.

It is important to note that the private school student and the public school student have the same federal protections. The private school student has a right to the same services a public school student is entitled to receive. However, the private school student may not be able to insist that the services be provided within a private school as part of an IEP.

REQUIREMENTS OF EDUCATION ACCESS LAWS

The *Americans with Disabilities Act* (ADA), like Section 504 of the *Rehabilitation Act of 1973*, also requires that disabled persons be offered reasonable accommodations, those which an institution could be expected to fund. It would not be reasonable to suppose that a Catholic school should institute a special program, with special teachers, for a blind student or a profoundly mentally handicapped student. Religious education programs could not be required to make all necessary accommodations for a deaf and blind catechist. There is an exemption in the ADA for religious institutions, and religious education and youth ministry programs are clearly part of a religious institution. Arguments can certainly be made that Catholic schools are as well, although the exact meaning of the statute has yet to be defined. Nonetheless, basic justice requires that, as far as possible, Catholic schools and programs attempt to make reasonable accommodations.

Neither Section 504 of the *Rehabilitation Act of 1974* nor the *Americans with Disabilities Act* requires that institutions create programs to meet the needs of the disabled. What these laws require is that institutions not discriminate against otherwise qualified persons who are seeking admission to their programs. If a disabled person can participate in the program with a reasonable amount of accommodation, then the institution must provide the accommodation. If providing that accommodation would create a significant hardship, the institution will not have to provide it. For example, if a blind student were to seek admission and acceptance of that student would require that a special teacher be employed for the student and that all teachers learn Braille, the school would probably not be expected to incur those expenses.

It must be frankly stated, however, that simply because one is not legally required to do something, it does not follow that one should not do that thing, if it is the *right* thing to do. If a school or parish has significant assets and could afford a sign language interpreter for a deaf student or instructions in signing for the faculty and staff, the educator may have a moral and ethical duty to provide for the student, even though the law does not require such provision. Indeed, *Welcome and Justice for Persons with Disability*, the pastoral statement on handicapped people of the U.S. Catholic Bishops issued in 1978, seems to demand such action: "If handicapped people are to become equal partners in the Christian community, injustices must be eliminated." Certainly, Catholic parishes and schools should be leaders in fighting injustice wherever it is found, especially as it affects those whose disabilities place them among persons for whom Christ manifested special concern.

THE RIGHT TO THE BEST EDUCATION

All students have the right to a "free and appropriate education" according to *Public Law 94-142*, the *Education of All Handicapped Children Act*, as noted above. Students must be evaluated for special services at parental request, but the law does not entitle students to a special needs program. Catholic school students have the same right to evaluation that public school students have. However, the program recommended as a result of the evaluation may not be available in the Catholic school, which is required only to make reasonable accommodations.

Discrimination law requires that students receive a "free and appropriate" education, but it does not require that the education be the best available. To require the best education would mean that school systems would constantly be meeting parental demands for instructional services that could "better" student performance.

As a result of case law that overturned the 1985 *Aguilar v. Felton* decision, public schools can now provide services in religious schools. The key word is *can*, which is not synonymous with *must*. Thus, public schools could still refuse to provide services in Catholic schools so long as the students have access to them in the public schools.

Much apprehension could be alleviated if administrators clearly understood what the law does and does not require. In the final analysis, though, the question is not, "Did you do what you had to do?" but "Did you do what you could?"

STANDARDS OF SUPERVISION AND DISCIPLINE

Board members and administrators, many of whom are familiar with the adage, "the younger the child chronologically or mentally, the greater the standard of care," may well ask: "If we accept students with special needs, are we committing ourselves to higher levels of supervision?"

Teachers and other adult supervisors can be held to different standards. For example, a teacher who is supervising a senior honors class probably will be held to a lower standard than an individual teaching kindergarten children. Courts assume that older children can be expected to take some responsibility for themselves.

Mental age is concerned with the effect that a disability may have on a child. If a Catholic school accepts a student with a mental disability, teachers must make reasonable accommodations. If a child performs well below grade level and exhibits immature behavior, a teacher may be expected to provide more stringent supervision than that given to other students. Some disabilities are not mental, of course. If a child is an amputee, the child will require more supervision and help in physical activities than others may need.

Although this author knows of no case in which a court has ruled that a parish program must accommodate disabilities, the possibility of liability is always present, if not now, then in the future. Surely, the more important question is: "How would Jesus want us to treat persons with special needs?" Discussion of this question can be difficult, particularly in light of rising costs and limited personnel. At some point, all involved in Catholic education need to examine their institutional responses to special needs. If individual parishes and schools cannot meet needs, can something be done collectively?

DISCIPLINE

All students need to be accountable to persons in authority, and special needs children are no exception. Schools and parishes have the right to require that all students abide by codes of conduct. Every student in a Catholic institution should be expected to obey the rules.

Exceptions are in order only when the infraction is the result of the disability. If students who use walkers or crutches cannot get to class on time because they simply cannot move fast enough, it would be unfair to penalize them for being late. Another example is presented by a student with Tourette's syndrome, which is often characterized by bizarre behavior such as swearing. If a student suffering from Tourette's were to use profanity, it would be unfair to discipline the student if the behavior is beyond the student's control.

CASE LAW

In one case under the *Individuals with Disabilities in Education Act*, the United States District Court for the Southern District of Texas held that the parents of a hearing impaired student were not entitled to reimbursement from the public school district for their unilateral change of their child to a private program. The parents disagreed with the particular program that the Individual Education Plan offered the student. The parents argued that since they did not believe that the public school program offered their child the best possible education, they should be allowed to enroll their child in the school they believed provided the best program. Further, the parents claimed that the public school district was legally bound to reimburse them for the cost of the private school tuition. However, the student was making progress in an appropriate manner in the public school program in which she had been enrolled; thus, the court found that no reimbursement was in order. See *Bonnie Ann F. by John. R. v. Calallen Independent School District*, S.D. Tex., Civ. No. C-91-259 (1993).

In a similar case, *Doe by and through Doe v. Board of Education of Tullahoma City Schools*, C.A.Tenn., No. 92-5996 (1993), a federal appeals court held that a student's IEP met the standards of the *Individuals with Disabilities Education Act*. The student suffered from a neurological impairment which hindered his ability to process auditory information and use normal language and thinking skills. The IEP offered mainstreaming with a provision for oral, rather than written examinations, and tutorial assistance. Although the parents contested the IEP, the court found that an appropriate education was being provided. Thus, the court declined to require the school board to reimburse parents for private tuition when they removed the student to a private program.

Both cases indicate that courts are reluctant to require reimbursement for private school tuition if the program developed for a special needs student seems to provide an "appropriate" public education. Catholic education administrators should be wary of any parent of a special needs student who claims that a public school district will pay tuition.

CHRISTIAN CONCERN

Children and adolescents with special needs are certainly worthy of the Catholic Church's time and attention. It is a sad reality that only a few schools and parishes make adequate provisions for meeting the needs of such children. As persons striving to live in harmony with the Gospel, all involved in Catholic education are bound to do their utmost to assist students with special needs.

Two suggestions seem appropriate with regard to special education in the day-to-day operation of a school or program. Administrators should treat parents the way they would want to be treated if they had special needs children. No parent should ever be told on the telephone or by letter, "Sorry, there's no place for your child here." At the very least, administrators should offer to meet with such parents and discuss the situation. Even if a particular school or program cannot accommodate a child's needs, the administration will have expressed Christian concern.

Another suggestion is that all school and program administrators commit to undertaking an analysis of their programs' ability to meet special needs. An inability to meet special needs is not synonymous with inconvenience.

Jesus ordered his disciples, "Let the children come to me. For such is the kingdom of heaven." Such is the mission of all Catholic educators—to be as inclusive as Jesus was.

REFLECTION/DISCUSSION QUESTIONS
1. Teachers in your Catholic school are concerned about a certain situation, and the principal has agreed to bring the matter before the school board for its discussion. A student with diagnosed learning disorders told a teacher that he will be taping classes from now on "because the doctor said it would help." Some teachers are afraid that the student's parents have another agenda—gathering evidence against the teacher. The principal asks your advice, "Should she comply with the taping request or not?"
2. The principal has brought a "problem" case to the board for advice. Mrs. K, who already has two children in your school and one who has graduated, has asked the school to admit her daughter who is totally blind. She says it will be no problem for the school to have materials translated into Braille and that student helpers can be

assigned to her daughter to assist her in getting around the building. Do you think the school should accept this student? Why or why not? What legal issues do you see?

3. Mr. Brown, who has contributed several hundred thousand dollars to the recent building fund, has asked that the board consider the religious education program's lack of provisions for young persons with disabilities. His young grandson has been diagnosed with autism. He and the child's parents want the son, who is a first grader, in the regular program. The child rarely speaks and engages in distracting repetitive behavior. Mr. Brown says that he will pay for any training that staff members need. He is distressed because the DRE refused to consider the matter. What do you think the board should do?

12

Extracurricular and Cocurricular Activities

Extracurricular and cocurricular activities have long been a part of schools, but members of boards that do not have responsibilities for schools may believe the topic has little relevance for them. Yet most parish programs involve community service experiences, and may involve other activities such as speech and debate clubs, athletic games/intramurals, and choir recitals, to name a few. With these activities comes an increased concern for legal issues.

A busy administrator or activity sponsor often notices some problems with an activity and decides that next year will be different. Adults who sponsor extracurricular activities will understand their various responsibilities and will conscientiously perform their duties. Academic and behavioral requirements for extracurricular participation will be published to all persons involved, and these mandates will be enforced. Some plan for dealing with young persons who are dropped off for practices or activities well before an adult supervisor is present or who are still on campus long after activities have concluded will be in place. However, as any seasoned educator knows, next year comes all too soon.

As the school or program year comes to a close, faculty and staff should be involved in the development of a plan for improvement of the programs offered. Staff members should be encouraged to submit their suggestions in writing. The administrator and moderator can schedule times to meet to determine policies and procedures for the coming year.

By their very nature, extracurricular and cocurricular activities are more dangerous than ordinary classroom experiences. Participants and their parents can appear to care far more passionately about extracurricular programs than about curriculum offerings. An angry student or parent can threaten a lawsuit. The reasonable educator will not be unduly alarmed when threats are made. If policies and procedures are properly developed and implemented, the administrator will be in the best possible position.

This chapter will address three areas of legal concerns in relation to extracurricular activities: the assignment and training of moderators, student selection and standards for participation, and administrative monitoring.

ASSIGNMENT OF MODERATORS

The absence of a moderator, either at the opening of school or during the year, can present a crisis situation for the administrator. There is a great temptation to take anyone who expresses interest in the activity and make that person the moderator. Such a procedure is particularly dangerous in athletics. While a person does not need to be an expert wrestler to coach wrestling or an outstanding actor to direct the play, the individual should be willing to study the requirements for coaching a team or directing a play. At the same time, persons who played a sport or acted in a play may believe that they can direct the activity when, in fact, participation does not guarantee the ability to teach another the skill.

Administrators must ensure that persons who moderate activities possess at least minimum understanding of the activity. For example, released time or other incentives can be provided to allow a neophyte moderator to visit a more experienced one or to choose a mentor at another school or parish. Such actions may be time-consuming, but they provide the best protection for the safety of students and the best defense against liability in the case of injury.

The applicant's experience and qualifications to serve as a moderator must be verified. If one has no actual experience through participating in the activity, one should be able to indicate how one has or will acquire the necessary knowledge or skills. If the moderator appears to be truly inexperienced and untried, that individual should not be assigned complete responsibility for the students participating in the activity, but could be assigned as an assistant to a more experienced faculty member.

Educators and board members may ask whether using a volunteer as a moderator is ever advisable. There are certainly times and occasions when such an action is the best possible one to take. If someone's mother had extensive experience directing college musicals, she may be able to direct the school or religious education play; she may even be more qualified to do so than anyone on the faculty. A student's father who was a football captain and coach of a town league may be able to serve as an outstanding coach. While the use of volunteers is certainly legally acceptable, the principal or other administrator must ensure that the individual is a person of integrity and trustworthiness. Some states require fingerprinting before individuals are allowed to work with young persons on a regular basis. At the very least, the administrator should ask for references and check them. In too many instances, persons with charming personalities and tendencies to pedophilia have been assigned to positions of great trust. While no one can avert every possible tragedy, the wise administrator will have some procedure in place to gather the necessary background information concerning volunteers.

Diocesan and/or local administrators should consider an annual orientation for extracurricular moderators. Athletic coaches may be offered a separate orientation. In the unfortunate event of a student injury, administrators must be able to demonstrate that they had taken their responsibilities seriously and had tried to ensure that moderators and coaches were competent.

STUDENT SELECTION STANDARDS

Most administrators have been the recipients of parent and/or student complaints regarding nonselection for an activity. Administrators should insist that moderators and coaches develop, publish, and implement clear standards for selection. Obviously, selection is a subjective process, and feelings can be hurt. The administrator who insists on clear standards and monitors the performance of moderators and coaches can be satisfied that the requirements of fairness are met. The administrator should guard against taking the side of a parent or student in a dispute over selection for, or retention in, an activity unless the moderator/coach is clearly in the wrong. One of the more difficult situations for a moderator and administrator is one in which the administrator "second guesses" the decisions of the moderator. An even more difficult situation arises when a board member tries to intervene. Boards study, recommend, and evaluate policies, but members should not become involved in the implementation of policies or in specific decisions made.

Each activity and each moderator will have some rules and regulations to which the student participant must adhere. Some may be general school rules; others may be specific to the activity. Further, in the case of athletics and drama, for example, state associations may provide other standards.

Rules and regulations should be standardized as far as possible. Is it fair for an athlete with a failing grade to be "benched," while another student with a similar grade is allowed to sing the lead in the school musical? Justice demands that everyone who participates in extra-curricular activities should abide by some common code of conduct.

Some rules and regulations that put conditions on participation might include: class attendance during the day of the activity, academic requirements (minimum grade averages, for example), and behavior requirements.

ADMINISTRATIVE MONITORING

Administrators need to be familiar with the rules and regulations of every activity in their schools or programs. Certainly they cannot be expected to recall every rule at any given moment, but they should have access to every rule and be able to obtain a copy of the rules if they cannot summon them from memory.

Administrators need to be physically present at athletic events and other extracurricular activities. No principal, DRE, or youth minister should be expected to be at every game or activity. Nevertheless, chief administrators should ensure that there is some administrative supervision in the course of the year. Regular meetings with moderators and coaches can also keep everyone informed and help to minimize problems.

REFLECTION QUESTIONS

1. The principal has asked you, a very active board member with three children in the school, to become the moderator of the fencing club. You have never fenced in your life. The principal insists that all you have to do is be present at practices and games, that you don't need to know anything about fencing. How will you respond?

2. The DRE presents the following information and asks for the board's advice. Every year a noted director of musicals in the city has directed a student performance in an adaptation of the Passion Play. This year the DRE had to find another director because the former director retired and moved to the Virgin Islands. Now the parents of student Q have complained to the DRE that Q did not get a major role. The parents state that last year's director promised that Q would get a big part if Q took acting lessons from him at the rate of $50 an hour. The parents want Q to have a major part or to be refunded the $2,000 spent on acting lessons. What advice will you give the DRE?

13

Athletics

Athletics, among all extracurricular activities, pose some of the greatest legal risks to parish and school programs. Principals, other administrators, athletic directors, and teachers constantly ask themselves how they can best protect student athletes from injury, and parishes and schools from liability.

AVOIDING NEGLIGENCE

Most lawsuits alleging negligence begin in the classroom, since that is where students spend most of their time. Other areas, however, are potentially more dangerous than the classroom, and exact a greater standard of care from staff and administrators. Athletic activities are clearly more dangerous than normal classroom activities.

As discussed earlier in this text, negligence is an unintentional act or omission that results in injury. Persons who bring successful negligence suits are usually awarded financial damages in an amount calculated to compensate for the actual injury suffered. Punitive or exemplary damages can also be awarded. In assessing whether a person's behavior is negligent, a court will use the "reasonable person" test: Would a reasonable person in the defendant's situation have acted in this manner? "Reasonable" is whatever the jury or other fact-finder decides it is.

Before a court will find a defendant legally negligent, four elements, previously discussed in chapter 3, must be present: *duty, violation of duty, proximate cause,* and *injury.* An examination of each of the four elements as applied to athletics should prove helpful to persons supervising athletic programs.

Duty to supervise. The individual charged with negligence must have a duty in the situation. Student athletes have a right to safety; coaches and other officials have a responsibility to protect the well-being of all those entrusted to their care. Coaches are assumed to have a duty to provide reasonable supervision of their players. It is expected that principals and athletic directors will have developed and promulgated rules and regulations which guide coaches in providing for student safety. Coaches should develop and implement team practices that are consistent with safety and in harmony with administrative practices.

Violation of duty. Negligence cannot exist if the second element, violation of duty, is not present. Courts understand that accidents and spontaneous actions can occur. The 1989 New York case, *Benitez v. NYC Board of Education*, 543 N.Y. 2d 29, involved a high school football player who was injured during play. The player alleged negligence on the part of the coach and principal for allowing him to play while he was fatigued.

A lower court awarded the student damages, but the appellate court ruled that school officials had to provide only reasonable, not extraordinary, care and reversed the decision. Further, the court invoked the doctrine of *assumption of the risk*. Students are under no compulsion to play sports. If they choose to participate, they voluntarily assume the risks of some injuries. Assumption of the risk is a defense against an allegation of negligence.

At first glance, it may appear that athletic directors and coaches are the officials who would be found liable for violation of duty in the case of student injury. Under the previously mentioned doctrine of *respondeat superior*, let the superior answer, principals and administrators can be found liable for the acts of subordinates. For example, if a principal or youth minister paid little or no attention to the administration of the athletic program, provided no supervision, and/or offered no guidance, he or she might well be found guilty of negligence if a student were to be injured while a dangerous practice or policy was in place. Unfortunately, many administrators believe themselves to be ignorant of the principles of athletics and are content to let coaches and athletic directors run the whole sports program unsupervised. These same administrators would be shocked if someone were to suggest that a second-year English teacher is an expert, needs no supervision, and should be given *carte blanche* in directing his or her classes.

Principals and other program administrators have an obligation to oversee athletics, while teachers and staff must support the regulation of the athletic program. Certainly, no one expects an administrator to be an athletic expert, but the administrator should be sure that only qualified individuals are hired as coaches and athletic directors. The administrator should insist that athletic directors and/ or coaches keep both administrators and staff members informed about the operation of the program.

Every administrator and athletic director should seriously consider having an athletic handbook outlining the policies and procedures for each sport. Parents and students should sign a statement agreeing to be governed by the provisions of the handbook.

Administrators will not be held responsible for every mistake of employees and volunteers, but only for those that a reasonable person could have foreseen. In the 1979 Virginia case *Short v. Griffits*, 255 S.W.2d 479, an athletic director was held liable for injuries sustained by a student who fell on broken glass while running laps. The school and the school board were exonerated. It was the athletic director's responsibility to ensure that the playing areas and equipment were in order. Unless the principal had some reason to believe that the employee was careless in supervision, the principal would not be expected to check the area for hazards.

Proximate cause. The third requirement for legal negligence is that the violation of duty must be the proximate cause of the injury. Proximate cause is sometimes defined as a contributing factor. If a coach were to order a 250-pound student to wrestle a 125-pound student and the lighter student were injured in the match, the coach is the proximate cause of the injury, even though the physical actions of the heavier student are the direct cause of the injury.

The court must decide whether proper performance of duty could have prevented the injury and, in so doing, the court has to look at the facts of each individual case. In an old, but still applicable 1970 case, *Stehn v. MacFadden Foundations*, 434 F2d 811 (U.S.C.A. 6th Cir.), a private school and its officials were held liable for damages sustained by a student who suffered a severe spinal cord injury in a wrestling match. The court found that the maneuver which resulted in the injury was not listed in any reputable book on the subject of teaching wrestling, and the defense could produce no evidence that the maneuver was legitimate. The coach had very limited previous experience and was coaching without any supervision.

The court ruled that the school's violation of duty, its failure to ensure that the coach was qualified and experienced, was the proximate cause of the student's injury. Proximate cause is a complex doctrine, so it can be difficult to predict what a court will determine to be the proximate cause in any particular allegation of negligence.

Injury. The fourth element necessary for a finding of negligence is injury. To prevail in a lawsuit, a student must have sustained an injury for which the court can award a remedy. No matter how unreasonable the behavior of a coach, there is no legal negligence if there is no injury. Everyone must understand, however, that physical harm is not the only type of injury; emotional or psychological harm can also constitute injury.

Even if every possible precaution were taken, the possibility for student injury while participating in athletics is very high. Educators have a real duty to ensure that only competent personnel—trained in coaching techniques, theory of the sport, and first aid/safety procedures—are employed. Additional policies should provide:

- Clear procedures to be followed when accidents occur
- Minimal delay in seeking medical attention when needed
- Hazard-free equipment and playing areas

While there is no absolute protection against lawsuits, particularly in athletics, a thorough handbook, as indicated above, can provide the best possible protection. It can serve as evidence that both parents and students understand the risks involved in sports and the requirements of participation in the school athletic program.

GRADING AND EXCLUSION FROM ATHLETICS

Educators often face the problem of students who just barely miss attaining the necessary minimum grades to continue participation in a sport. Students, parents, and others can exert considerable pressure on teachers to change grades so that students can qualify to play. One might argue that such a practice is hardly the material of which lawsuits are made. Even if no lawsuit is ever filed, issues of fairness deserve consideration.

REFLECTION QUESTIONS
1. If asked, how would you describe the role of athletics (formal or informal) in your school or program? Are there areas where board members can offer guidance and policy development?
2. Student M, the star volleyball player, asks her teacher to give her one extra point on her grade so she won't be suspended from the team and miss tournament play. She offers to do extra work. Without M, there is very little chance that the team can win any of the tournament games, and indeed the team lost its first match. The board chair has just received a phone message from M's father, the chief justice of the state supreme court, asking for an opportunity to address the board. He says he has already tried talking to the teacher and principal. Although she missed the invitational tournament, the student's father wants to be sure that the teacher gives her the point in time for the state tournament. He wants a board decision by 8:00 tomorrow morning. What should the board do?

14

Personal Conduct
of Professional Staff

Issues of actual or perceived inappropriate staff conduct often confront board members and administrators. What legal rights do they have to demand certain standards of behavior from staff members, particularly during off-campus times? Clearly, what a staff member does, both in and out of the educational setting, impacts the quality and integrity of ministry within the setting. The doctrine of separation of church and state protects administrators of religiously sponsored schools and programs and allows them to set standards of personal behavior that would not be permitted in the public sector.

BEHAVIORAL EXPECTATIONS FOR CATHOLIC EDUCATORS

Board members should ensure that documents governing employment state that staff members' behavior is expected to support the teachings of the Catholic Church. Obviously, many programs have non-Catholic staff members, and one would not expect such individuals to attend Mass outside the school on a regular basis or to be participating members of a parish. Nevertheless, non-Catholics who seek to acquire or retain positions in Catholic settings should expect that relevant standards of behavior would be in force. For example, if the fact that an individual had an abortion becomes known and is a source of scandal, the school and/or parish has every right to terminate that individual's employment or volunteer status. To do otherwise might send a confusing message to parents, students, and the larger community.

ISSUES OF SEXUAL PREFERENCE AND/OR LIFESTYLE

Issues of sexual preference pose special problems. While no one should condemn a homosexual orientation, a Catholic educational administrator, as an agent of the church, cannot ignore gay lifestyle manifestations that pose scandal.

Equally difficult decisions must be made in situations involving divorced staff members who remarry without an annulment if that fact becomes known. There is no easy solution, but board members and administrators have an obligation to see that the teachings of the Catholic Church are respected and not compromised in the witness given by staff members. Many diocesan policies are concerned with scandalous public behavior, and board members should use diocesan policies as a basis for parish and school policies.

Once an individual performs an act that is inconsistent with church teaching and becomes publicly known, that person may no longer be qualified to minister in a given situation at that time. While such a reality may seem obvious, it is recommended that documents state the requirement of supporting the teachings of the church.

ILLEGAL ACTIVITY

A person who has committed an illegal act may certainly have employment or volunteer status terminated. One who is convicted of, or who admits commission of, a crime should be removed from professional and/or volunteer status. The harder question arises when a person is simply accused of, or arrested on suspicion of, a crime. Board members and administrators may be sharply divided as to the proper response to make in such a situation.

The United States has long operated under the principle of "innocent until proven guilty." It may appear that until guilt is established, the fair approach would be to let the person continue in ministry. Yet the reality often is that effectiveness in such situations is severely compromised.

How, then, should one deal with an arrest of, or serious accusation concerning, a staff member? Every educational entity should have a policy in place that allows the administrator to place the accused individual on a leave of absence pending the outcome of an investigation or an adjudication of guilt. The time to enact a policy is *not* when it is needed. The prudent administrator and educational board will have policy in place that anticipates such situations.

RELATIONSHIPS WITH STUDENTS

An earlier chapter discussed the legal risks posed by student/staff relationships. Obviously, teachers and staff members want to demonstrate a personal interest in their students. It is a sad reality, however, that board members and administrators must be vigilant in monitoring staff behavior in an effort to avoid even the appearance of impropriety.

While realizing the complexity inherent in many of the situations discussed above, both board members and administrators must ensure that fidelity to the church and compliance with the law characterize policies and procedures. The teacher or staff member must support the teachings of the Catholic Church.

REFLECTION QUESTIONS

1. The administrator has asked the board chair to convene a special meeting. She is extremely concerned that a 22-year-old male fifth grade teacher (or catechist) is a frequent visitor to gay bars, intends to march in a gay rights parade, and has told a few people that he will soon wed his male lover in an ancient Druid ceremony. The administrator has not been able to confirm any of these rumors. No policy directly addresses the situation. How will you, as a board member, advise the administrator?

2. You are a school board member. You have just learned that the fifth-grade teacher has a 10-year-old conviction for child abuse. You have heard that the victim intends to call a press conference and expose the teacher. At the time of his sentencing, he was told that if he successfully completed probation, his record would be expunged. (Please do not discuss whether expunging such a record is right or wrong.) He met the requirements and the record was expunged. According to existing law at that time, a person with expunged records could truthfully answer that he or she had never been convicted of a crime. The teacher is extremely popular and very generous, with no suggestion of scandalous behavior on his part. What, if anything, should the board and/or administration do? Why?

3. It has come to the DRE's attention that a 25-year-old male catechist has become quite interested in his 15 third-grade students. He has told them all that he will come to visit everyone in their homes at some time. He plans to just drop in. If the parents are home, fine; if not, he will just visit with the child. What should the DRE do? Why?

15

Gangs

In the last decade or so, the word "gang" has taken on a very different meaning than it had 20, 30, or 50 years ago. Many readers remember their parents or grandparents referring to the good times they had while they "ran around with a gang of friends." Today, the word has a sinister connotation of fear, violence, and domination. Suddenly, everyone is clamoring for schools and parishes to do something about the presence and activities of gangs, and many dioceses are writing and implementing policies concerning them.

DEFINITION

The first step in developing policy is to define exactly what a gang is. A 1991 California case, *The People v. Ralph Gamez*, 235 Cal. App. 3d 957, was significant in its definition of gangs. The court stated that the proper term to use when discussing problematic gangs is "criminal gang-like behavior." Unless one's state law has a different term or definition, diocesan staff and/or local administrators would be well-advised to adopt such a designation.

An analysis of *Gamez* and similar cases leads to a clearer definition of criminal gang-like activity. The archdiocese of Louisville, Kentucky, offers this definition: "Criminal gang-like activity involving membership in a criminal gang is defined as an ongoing organization, association, or group of three or more persons, whether formal or informal, having as one of its primary activities the commission of one or more criminal acts." Thus, both educator and young person should understand that the intent to commit criminal acts is what distinguishes criminal gang-like activity from other types of group activities. Moreover, it is not membership in a gang in and of itself that is the problem; it is the criminal activity.

Some persons may be tempted to think that enumerating all possible criminal offenses is useful in policy writing. In actuality, the issue of gangs is one that is better dealt with in general rather than specific terms. The term "criminal-like gang activity" includes all possible offenses. Attempts to enumerate them can result in the omission of some or an argument by an aggrieved student that what he or she did was not "terroristic threatening" or "property damage," for example.

GANG ATTIRE

The wearing of colors has long indicated membership in a gang. Any parish is well within its rights to forbid such displays. However, it is not always easy to identify the display of gang colors. In one state, for example, the athletic teams at two universities wear their different school colors. Gang members wear a particular university's sweatshirts, jackets, and so on, to denote their membership in a particular gang. Certainly there is nothing wrong with wearing a college sweatshirt, and it is very difficult, if not impossible, to determine who is supporting a team and who is displaying gang colors. Many public schools now require students to wear uniforms. While the constitutionality of this mandate has yet to be tested, one result is a lessening of the wearing of gang colors. Catholic educators should enforce uniform regulations and/or dress codes and be attentive to violations of the codes.

DISCIPLINARY STEPS

If a teacher, catechist, youth minister, or other staff member suspects or notices criminal gang-like activity at any time during educational and related activities, the principal or other chief administrator should be notified immediately.

The administrator should seek appropriate advice concerning investigation of the suspicion or allegation and then proceed to gather necessary data. If the administrator determines or strongly suspects that the young person is involved in criminal gang-like activity, his or her parents or guardians should be notified and disciplinary action taken as appropriate. In the case of suspicion without any convincing evidence, a warning concerning the consequences for anyone who engages in criminal gang-like activity may be given. Written documentation of any meetings should be kept.

If a criminal act has occurred, the administrator has a legal responsibility to notify local law enforcement officials and to assist the officials as far as possible in their investigation.

An educator should focus on what was actually done that is/was wrong, rather than on membership in a gang. If a school rule has been broken, the breaking of the rule should be discussed and appropriate sanctions given. If a crime has been committed, the focus should be on the crime and its consequences.

Sometimes young people need help to avoid or terminate membership in a gang. Counselors should have some training or know where to contact trained persons so that students can be helped to avoid gangs.

The days of simply announcing that some activity or association is wrong and expecting immediate student compliance are gone. It is every educator's responsibility to help in the creation of a community in which persons have no desire to engage in criminal gang-like activity.

REFLECTION QUESTIONS

1. If your parish or school has a gang policy, do you believe it is adequate? Why or why not? If there is no policy, do you think one should be developed or implemented? What do you think should be included in the policy?

2. When visiting your daughter, student H asks if she can talk with you. She tells you that she is "in deep" with a gang whose members are planning a series of house robberies over the weekend. H says she has seen the guns the gang intends to use. H wants out of the gang, but fears bodily harm if she leaves. She asks your advice. You know that the board has been intending to write a policy, but currently does not have one. What do you say and do?

16

Copyright Law, Technology, and Cyberspace

M ost persons realize that copyright law exists, and many would probably agree that rules should be followed when making copies of articles, book chapters, computer programs, and television programs. Teachers and other staff members have seen notices warning persons using copy machines that they are subject to the provisions of the copyright law.

For some individuals, the fact that few persons are apprehended and prosecuted for breaking the copyright law becomes a license to break the law. For others, the desire to help students and young people learn is an excuse for failing to comply with the law.

In his book on fair use, Merickel observed: "Although this act [copying] may appear innocent on the surface, copyright infringement, whether malicious or not, is a criminal act. One's position as a teacher and having 'only the best interests of your students at heart' does not give anyone the right to copy indiscriminately."[7]

In the 1960s and 1970s, budgetary considerations were the reasons given by Catholic parishes that copied songs from copyrighted works and used the copies to compile parish hymnals. Courts have consistently struck down such uses and have ordered the offending churches to pay damages.

Today, parishes appear to be aware of the legal consequences of copying and many subscribe to the licensing arrangements of music companies. For a given sum of money, the institution can make as many copies of music as desired during the span of the contract.

However, some teachers and catechists still copy items such as whole workbooks, other consumable materials, and large portions of books and print materials. The swift advance of technology has catapulted computer programs, videocassettes, and similar media into the sphere of copying.

COPYRIGHT LAW

This section will discuss copyright law as it applies to educators and educational institutions, examines the tests of "fair use," and offers some guidelines for board members and educators.

Upon reflection, most board members and administrators would agree that copyright protection is a just law. Both the *Copyright Act of 1909* (the old law) and the *Copyright Act of 1976* (the new law) represent attempts to safeguard the rights of authors. Persons who create materials are entitled to the fruits of their labors, and those who use author's creations without paying royalties, buying copies, or seeking permission are guilty of stealing.

Educators and the law. It is tempting to think that copyright infringements and lawsuits are more or less the exclusive domain of large institutions. Certainly the public learns about large-scale abuses faster than individual abuses. If a company is going to sue someone, it will seek a person or institution that has been guilty of multiple infringements so that larger damages can be won. It simply doesn't make good economic sense to sue someone who will be ordered to pay only a small amount of damages.

Sometimes, though, lawsuits are brought solely to prove a point. A 1983 case, *Marcus v. Rowley*, 695 F2d 1171, involved a dispute between two teachers in the same school. One teacher had prepared and copyrighted a 20-page booklet on cake decorating; the second teacher copied approximately half the pages and included them in her own materials. The amount of money involved was negligible; the author had sold fewer than 100 copies at a price of $2 each. Nonetheless, the court found the second teacher guilty of copyright violation; her use of the other's materials was not "fair."

Fair use. Section 107 of the *1976 Copyright Act* deals with "fair use" and specifically states that the fair use of copies in teaching "is not an infringement of copyright."

The sticking point is what the term fair use means. The section lists four factors to be included in any determination of fair use:

- The purpose and character of the use, including whether such use is of a commercial nature or is for nonprofit educational purposes
- The nature of the copyrighted work
- The amount and substantiality of the portion used in relation to the copyrighted work as a whole
- The effect of the use upon the potential market for or value of the copyright work

Educators should have little or no trouble complying with the "purpose and character of the work" factor. Teachers and catechists generally copy materials to aid the educational process. It should be noted, however, that recreational use of copied materials such as video-cassettes or computer games is generally not allowed under the statute.

"The nature of the copyrighted work" factor can prove a bit more problematic than "character and purpose of the work." Who determines what is the nature of the work—the creator and/or copyright holder, the person making the copies, the judge and/or the jury? Almost any material can be classified as educational in some context; even a cartoon can be found to have some educational purpose if one is willing to look for it. It seems reasonable that, in determining nature, a court would look to the ordinary use of the work and to the author's intent in creating the work.

The "amount and substantiality" of the work copied is especially troublesome in the use of videocassettes and computer programs. Teachers, catechists, and others understand that they are not sup-posed to copy a whole book, but may not understand that copying a television program or a movie onto videotape or copying a com-puter program for student use can violate the "amount and substan-tiality" factor.

In the case of *Encyclopedia Britannica v. Crooks*, 542 F. Supp. 1156 (W.D.N.Y. 1982), an educational company engaged in copying commercially available tapes and television programs for teachers was found to be in violation of the *Copyright Act*. The company argued that it was providing an educational service for students and teachers who would otherwise be deprived of important educational opportunities. The court rejected the argument.

Educators may be tempted to think that their small-scale copying acts could not compare with the scope of the activities in this case. In the majority of instances involving single copying, there is no comparison. However, the relatively new practice of developing libraries of copies is emerging in some schools and religious education programs. Whether the collections are of print materials or nonprint materials, such as videotapes and computer programs, the practice of building collections can easily be subjected to the same scrutiny as the *Encyclopedia* case.

The last of the four factors, "effect on the market," is also difficult to apply in the educational setting. Arguments can be advanced that students would not rent or purchase commercially available items, even if the copies weren't available. It appears, though, that use of an author's work without appropriate payment for the privilege is a form of economic harm. Good faith generally will not operate as an acceptable defense in educational copyright or infringement cases.

In *Roy v. Columbia Broadcasting System*, 503 F. Supp. 1137 (S.D.N.Y. 1980) p. 1151, the court stated: "The federal copyright statute protects copyrighted works against mere copying, even when done in good faith and even when not done to obtain a competitive advantage over the owners of the copyright in the infringed works."

Guidelines. A congressional committee developed "Guidelines for Classroom Copying in Not-for-Profit Educational Institutions," printed in *House Report 94-1476*, 94th Congress 2d Sess. (1976). Administrators should ensure that staff members have access to copies of the guidelines, which are readily available from local libraries, the Copyright Office, and members of Congress. Although these guidelines do not have the force of law that the statute has, judges have used them in deciding cases. Some examples of the guidelines follow.

For poetry, the copying of a complete poem of less than 250 words printed on no more than two pages or of an excerpt of 250 words from a longer poem is allowed. For prose, a complete work of less than 2,500 words, or an excerpt from a longer work of not more than 1,000 words, or 10% of the work is permissible. The guidelines mandate that copying meets this test of *brevity*.

The copying must be *spontaneous*. The educator must have decided more or less on the spur of the moment to use an item. Spontaneity presumes that a person did not have time to secure permission for use from the copyright holder. A teacher or catechist who decides in September to use certain materials in December has ample time to seek permission. In such a situation, failure to seek permission means that the spontaneity requirement will not be met.

A last requirement is that the copying must not have a *cumulative effect*. Making copies of poems or songs by one author would have a cumulative effect and would mean that collected works of the author would not be bought. Similarly, as indicated above, the practice of "librarying" (building a collection of taped television programs, for example) is not permitted. Copying computer programs is never advisable, unless permission to make copies is included in the purchase or rental agreement.

Videotapes recorded from television may be kept for 45 days only. During the first 10 days, a teacher or other educator may use the tape once in a class (although there is a provision for one repetition for legitimate instructional review). For the remaining 35 days educators may use the tape for evaluative purposes only.

TECHNOLOGY CHALLENGES

Ten years ago most educators—and certainly most Catholic educators—had limited access to computer technology. Today it is hard to imagine life without computers and the related technology of the information age. Access to volumes of information that would have taken much time to gather a few years ago can now be obtained in a few moments with the aid of a modem and a database. These developments, as wonderful as they are, present challenges for the educator who seeks to act in ways that are morally, ethically, and legally correct.

Appropriateness of materials available. Headlines reveal that several young persons have run away from home as a result of propositions received from persons on the Internet. Currently no truly foolproof means of monitoring and/or censoring material exists on the Internet and other networks. There is nothing to prevent unsupervised young people from being in electronic conversation with inappropriate persons about sexual matters, drugs, crime, and other less than suitable topics. The growing popularity of chat rooms presents a particular ethical/moral dilemma. Since there are no privacy police, people who log into a chat room can write anything they wish to another person who is in the room at the same time. E-mail provides a means for persons with no prior knowledge of each other to share intimate conversation.

Chat rooms and E-mail present issues of morality not unlike those presented by television and movies. The television industry polices itself, at least to a degree. For example, one does not generally find prime-time pornography on the major networks. Although adult channels are available on cable TV, parents and other supervisors can purchase devices that allow them to block access to such channels. Hotels and motels allow parents to call the front desk and have access to movie channels blocked in their rooms.

The movie industry provides a rating system that indicates the appropriateness of content for certain age groups. The dearth of PG movies, however, indicates that movies without sex and violence do not generally sell as well as those containing such elements.

With no equivalent monitoring system in place in the world of cyberspace, parents, educators, and board members must maintain constant vigilance. Consumers need to lobby the computer industry to provide some means of evaluating content and limiting access. Some experts recommend the development of computer programs or microchips that will limit the availability of certain services. Voters need to lobby lawmakers to develop legislation that will provide protection for young persons. The First Amendment to the Constitution does permit much leeway in terms of expression, but it does not require that children and teenagers be given unlimited access to other persons' self-expression. Even if everyone else in the neighborhood is "surfing the Internet," adults must stand firm and monitor computer usage by the young people for whom they are responsible.

Policy development. Board members are responsible for developing policy regarding copyright law and technology, while principals and other administrators are responsible for supervision of all aspects of the educational process. If a person is charged with copyright violation, it is likely that the principal will be charged as well. Clear policies and careful monitoring of those policies can lessen exposure to liability. As many legal authorities have observed, copyright violation is stealing. It appears, then, that "Thou shalt not steal" remains good law. At the very least, board members should adopt a policy requiring compliance with copyright laws.

Board members and educators may be tempted to believe the often-quoted line from *The Merchant of Venice*, "To do a great right, do a little wrong." Ethical, moral, and legal imperatives do not accept such rationalization. Students, whether wealthy or not, have a right to experience the richness of technology. At the same time, they have a right to expect that adults will protect them from harm and will exercise vigilance over technological as well as other behaviors. Lastly, educators themselves must be models of integrity and observe the laws that grant authors and other creators the right to the fruits of their labors. Obviously, the Internet and the information highway were not part of Jesus' lived experience, but it is important to reflect on how he would want us to meet the challenges they present in today's world. Catholic educators must surely model their behavior on that of Jesus, who scrupulously paid the temple tax, rendered Caesar his due, and exhorted landowners to pay workers a generous wage.

REFLECTION QUESTIONS

1. Six students have just told the principal that Student I has been logging onto a chatroom (he managed to bypass the lock-out) and is planning to visit a 40-year-old woman he met on the "May/December Romance Hotline." The principal asks for the board members' advice. What will you say?

2. Assume no policies are in place governing the use of the Internet. How should the board research and develop policy? What policy elements do you believe are crucial?

3. The youth minister is planning a youth production of *Oklahoma*, but the licensing fee is very high. A friend of his has 20 copies of the librettos and scripts that he said the company didn't ask him to return. The friend offers to give them to the youth group. The youth minister asks you, a board member, if it would really be so bad to accept the copies since the youth ministry budget is severely strained. How will you respond?

17

Health Issues

A lthough persons in private institutions do not have the same constitutional protections as those in the public sector, statutory laws such as health regulations can bind both the public and private sectors. Board members, pastors, and other ministers should carefully read all health-related communications from state or local agencies. Administrators, who should know what the laws are, will be held to the same standard as persons in the public sector. Boards of education need to develop and promulgate policies concerning health issues that are grounded in sound legal theory and practice. Public agencies can and will assist upon request.

This chapter will discuss employment issues, HIV and AIDS status, universal precautions, substance abuse, and medication.

HEALTH-RELATED EMPLOYMENT ISSUES

Staff members may be required to produce documentation of health and/or a doctor's statement that the person does not pose a health threat for the community. For example, tuberculosis, a communicable disease, poses a distinct threat. Many but not all states require new teachers to have a tuberculin skin test and/or a chest X-ray to rule out the presence of tuberculosis before the teacher starts work. It seems appropriate that, whether required by law or not, teachers, other employees, and volunteers should be required to submit to tuberculosis testing at least once every five years.

HIV STATUS

Everyone involved in parish programs must understand that no one can be legally required to reveal personal HIV status or the fact that one has AIDS. If a student seeks admission to a parish program and has AIDS, that student and his or her parents do not have to inform the administrator. If the administrator discovers after enrollment that a student is infected, the student's enrollment status cannot be changed. The only exception is a situation in which a student displays behaviors, such as biting, that could pose problems for other students. These same principles apply to employing persons who have AIDS or who are HIV-positive. Board members need to ensure that school or program policy protects the rights of those who are HIV-positive as well as of those persons suffering from other communicable diseases.

UNIVERSAL PRECAUTIONS

Staff members should always use universal precautions whenever body fluids are present. No employee or volunteer dealing with children should be permitted to refuse to clean up body fluids or to render aid to a bleeding student. Boards of education must enact policies requiring the use of universal precautions. Clear procedures will help to ensure a calm, sound approach to situations involving body fluids.

The legal principle often applied in negligence cases, "the younger the child chronologically or mentally, the greater the standard of care," applies in body fluid situations. Although supervisors of small children are held to a higher standard, those who supervise older students are still held to the standard of taking whatever action a reasonable person would take.

SUBSTANCE ABUSE

Substance abuse is on the rise in America. Virtually no one is exempt from its effects. The American Medical Association has stated that substance abuse is an illness, not a moral weakness. Just as persons with other illnesses are protected by various disability laws, so too are substance abusers. A person's status may trigger disability protection, but that status cannot be used to excuse behavior contrary to rules. Consider a situation in which a teacher or youth minister keeps a bottle of vodka in her desk and is found drinking from it. From a disciplinary standpoint, the problem is one of inappropriate conduct, consuming liquor at work, not of being a substance abuser. Persons who abuse substances and agree to enter treatment are protected; those who refuse assessment and treatment are not.

DISPENSING MEDICATION

"I have to take my medicine," says the second-grader to the religious education secretary, who opens a cabinet reserved for student medications and begins to search for the appropriate bottle.

"I took this bottle of pills away from this student. It is a prescription and someone else's name is on the bottle," reports a catechist.

"Here are Mary's medications, plus a bottle of Tylenol and an over-the-counter cough syrup," declares the mother who opens a plastic bag and dumps medicine bottles on the secretary's desk.

How should staff respond? One of the more challenging tasks facing parish and school administrators today is the dispensing of medicine.

Few parishes and schools have nurses on their staffs. Board members and administrators must grapple with appropriate policies and procedures, which might include:

- All medication must be brought to the appropriate office with a parent's note.
- Only prescription medication can be brought and must be stored in a designated office.
- No over-the-counter medication is allowed unless a written doctor's authorization is submitted.
- Prescription medication must be in the original bottle with the student's name on it along with a parent's written permission.
- The parish and/or school will not dispense medication, so students or their parents are responsible for their own medication unless they are unable to medicate themselves.
- The parish does not dispense over-the-counter medication, so a parent must come to the school or program to administer the medication.
- Some variation of these approaches is developed.

It may appear that medication issues properly belong with school administrators, since parish programs are generally for a relatively short period of time. Still, the wise board will develop appropriate policies for all programs, even if those policies are never needed. It is far easier to develop a policy that is never used than it is to construct a policy after an incident occurs.

Opinions vary as to the best approach. Some medical professionals do not want to take time to write notes for over-the-counter prescriptions. Parents grumble about an extra trip to the doctor to get written authorization. Some high school programs expect students to be responsible for self-administering all medication.

Attorneys can identify problems with almost any approach. Whenever an official administers medication, he or she may be liable for any reaction that occurs. One dangerous policy allows parents to bring over-the-counter medications with the child's name written on it. The difficulty is that persons are having increasing problems with reactions to nonprescription medicine. In one case, a student was given a common over-the-counter drug; no one knew that the student had an allergy to the product, and he died.

The practice of parishes and schools storing parent-supplied over-the-counter medication appears to be growing. Even though written permission was on file, school and program officials have been sued for administering parent-supplied medication that interacted with some other medicine the student was taking. Some parents allege that the school or program should have recognized the possibility of drug interaction and should have asked questions concerning other medication. Several cases of this type are making their way through the judicial system. The need for policies and procedures is evident.

One question frequently asked in schools and programs which do not have nurses is: "Who should administer medication? The classroom teacher or catechist? The school or parish secretary? The principal, DRE, youth minister, or other administrator?" Although there is no one correct answer, board members and other decision makers should consider all options before designating persons as medication-givers.

The following statements offer some points to consider when policies and procedures are being determined.

1. The only persons who have an absolute right to the administration of medication are those who have serious chronic and/or

life-threatening illnesses. For example, those who are allergic to bee stings must have the antidote serum readily available. A diabetic must be able to have prescribed insulin injections. Diabetics can, of course, be taught to administer and monitor their own medication, while those allergic to bees most often need someone else to inject the antidote.

2. At least two persons must be identified who will be/are trained in the administration of injections or other drugs that a person cannot administer on his/her own.

3. Children and adolescents must be allowed to carry medication for life-threatening attacks. Asthma is one condition that may give no warning; if an inhaler is not immediately available, the student could be severely harmed.

4. Adults who administer medication must place their whole attention on the task. The proper paper work should be present, e.g., a prescription label in the student's name, a doctor's note of authorization, and a parent's written permission.

5. If a teacher, catechist, or youth minister has a student with a life-threatening disease, the adult must learn how to administer the medication. This reality is a matter of law, not choice.

6. Young children should not be responsible for oral medication, other than inhalers. Oral medication should be brought to, and kept in, the office.

7. High-school-age persons may be allowed to carry and monitor their own non-prescription medication, so long as the parent/student handbook contains a statement to that effect.

SUMMARY

Board members must understand that the school or parish that accepts possession of and responsibility for the administration of medications will be held to a very high standard of care. Certain cases warrant the administration of medication; in other cases, convenience rather than necessity appears to be the motivating factor. Educators generally are not medical professionals and boards of education must enact policies that will protect administrators and staff from unnecessary exposure to liability.

REFLECTION QUESTIONS

1. The DRE has requested a meeting of the religious education board regarding Mrs. Stone, a long-time parish member, who has brought seven bottles of prescription medication to the secretary's office for distribution to her daughter whenever she asks for it. All the medication is in properly labeled containers, along with a doctor's note stating that the student is on the medications. Board policy states that medication will be dispensed only when the student would suffer harm if it were not administered. Since religious education classes last only one hour, the DRE believes that it is unreasonable to request administration of medication. The DRE asks for direction. Do you have all the information you need? If not, how will you advise the DRE to get it? Based on the given facts alone, what do you think the DRE should do?

2. You are meeting a friend for lunch. The friend casually remarks that someone needs to do something about a hole in the girls' bathroom floor. Her daughter has tripped on it twice. When your friend asked the school principal to have it fixed, the principal replied that such repairs weren't in the budget and she had told all the students to be careful. The principal is sorry that the girl fell, but said that it is the student's responsibility to listen to announcements and warnings. Students who fall, says the principal, have only themselves to blame. What would you tell your friend? Would you do anything else? Why?

18

Setting Safety Policy

C atholic education board members have serious responsibilities for the safety of students and staff members. No member can afford to be unconcerned about any possible risk to safety.

Recent school shootings strike fear in the hearts of all persons responsible for children, teachers, and other members of the school/ parish community. The presence of criminal gangs and their attraction to youth may cause young people to behave in ways that a few decades ago would not have been imagined. Board members whose task it is to develop, recommend, and/or monitor implementation of policy are as concerned as anyone else in the school community.

To deal with the unthinkable, policies and procedures must be in place. Since boards recommend policies, they are one of the groups that must take a proactive stance. Board members cannot adopt a "wait and see" or "it will never happen here" attitude. There are far too many stories of student and staff injuries that could have been avoided if someone had been more aware of potential dangers. Catholic schools, as well as religious education and youth ministry programs, are targets for the mentally ill and for persons who decide to cause injury or death. Besides the tragedy that would occur if persons were killed or seriously injured, the school or parish would be in a risky legal position. Since the Catholic Church is already viewed as a rich and vulnerable organization, lawsuits in such situations would be almost inevitable. The parish and/or diocese would most likely face a civil negligence suit at best or criminal charges at worst. Thus, board members must ensure that facilities are safe and are continually monitored for problem areas. The following mechanisms can help to implement a proactive safety policy established by boards.

THREATS OF VIOLENCE

Policies should contain clear directives for dealing with threats of violence. While many adults grew up saying and hearing phrases such as "I'll kill you," these words cannot be ignored today. Every school or program must have a policy stating that all threats will be taken seriously. Students who make threats should be suspended and required to receive psychological assessment and counseling. The student can return only if he/she presents a written recommendation to that effect from the counselor, and the administration is willing to reenroll the student. If the student returns, his/her parents must be notified in writing that a second offense will result in automatic expulsion.

Although adults rarely make such threats, a policy should be in place for all employees and other adult community members that says if a threat is verified, the employee or volunteer is dismissed. Even parents can pose threats. In one Catholic elementary school, two mothers brought a fight to the school grounds. One woman went to her car, retrieved a butcher knife, and began threatening the other woman with it. Although another parent intervened and no one was hurt, the principal had to deal with the fact that the child's parent had brought to the school and threatened to use a deadly weapon. The next year the school had a policy. This situation illustrates the reality that policymakers must be proactive. No one can afford to wait until a policy is needed to write one. Board members must consider worst case scenarios and develop policies and procedures that can deal with them.

CRISIS MANAGEMENT PLAN

The board should ensure that a crisis management plan is in place and that everyone in the educational community is familiar with it. (National Catholic Educational Association has published an excellent book, *Crisis Management in Catholic Schools*,[8] which is an invaluable resource for boards and administrators.) All staff and students should participate in crisis drills. A code word or phrase such as, "Mr. Valentine, please come to the office," should alert staff to danger. Teachers and other staff members should require young persons to lie or sit on the floor while they lock the classroom door and lower any blinds or shades.

The parent/student handbook should apprise parents of any special procedures. For example, designated "safe places" such as stores or libraries should be established off campus and their management should agree that school members go there in case of an emergency, i.e., students and teachers released or able to escape from a crisis situation. (Supervising adults must understand that no unreasonable attempts to escape should be made.) A spokesperson and a process for dealing with media inquiries should also be determined.

SAFETY PLANS

The school/program should have an overall safety plan, including provisions for conducting an annual safety audit. At least one person conducting the audit should be a nonschool/nonparish employee qualified to give advice and make objective judgments and recommendations. The requirements of all civil laws and regulations must be met. Adult supervisors should be given a list of "do's and don'ts;" for example, adults should be instructed to refrain from chaining doors or blocking exits.

Everyone should be encouraged to foster safety in the school or parish. Students, parents, and employees should be able to offer constructive suggestions for safety improvements. An adult may not notice what is perfectly plain to a first grader. Involvement of all concerned parties is needed to ensure compliance and cooperation in setting and implementing safety policies. Much attention has been focused on violence and threatened violence, but there are warning signs that can often head off possible tragedy if teachers, catechists, and others pay attention to the signs and deal appropriately with them. Possible legal problems that can result from failure to heed signals are illustrated by the current lawsuits brought by the parents of school shooting victims. Such legal actions generally contend that the killer's papers contained dark allusions and alleged indications of a violent propensity but the teachers who read them did not take them seriously, and so student descent into violent behavior continued unabated.

At first glance, one may think that this type of lawsuit is doomed to failure. In the last five years or so, as indicated earlier in this text, courts have been considering such arguments in cases involving students who committed suicide after telling teachers in writing or orally that they intended such action. Several courts have indicated that teachers can be held liable for student death if they receive such information and fail to act on it. Administrators and board members must ensure that policy requires staff members to reveal confidential information if someone's health, life, and/or safety are at stake.

It is tempting to think that determining the appropriate response to "signals" is the province of the staff member and administrator. But those responsible for advising and setting policy have responsibilities, too. At least once a year, the board needs to review all policy statements; consider areas where addition, deletion or revision is appropriate; and recommend changes. With the rapid increase in litigation against schools, board members must consider the construction, maintenance, and monitoring of appropriate policy to be a primary obligation. Generally, if a lawsuit is filed against a parish and/or its programs, one of the major allegations will be that of negligence.

WHAT IS NEGLIGENCE?

The concept of legal negligence dates back to early English law. The theory is that if a person suffers harm resulting from another person's actions or inactions, the second person should be required to do whatever is necessary to make the first person "whole" again. Obviously, in cases involving debilitating injury or death, "wholeness" is not possible. In such instances, juries award damages in amounts calculated to compensate for injury. In making presentations across the country, this author has discovered that many teachers, administrators, and board members believe that lawsuits for negligence can be filed for any professionally inappropriate action, whether the action results in injury or not. Such a belief is erroneous, as the following discussion will illustrate.

Four elements must be present before a finding of legal negligence can be made, as indicated earlier. If even one of the four necessary elements of negligence—*duty, violation of duty, proximate cause,* or *injury*—is missing, the court must find that there is no legal negligence. Board members, like all involved in the educational ministries of the church, need to understand and be able to apply these concepts to various scenarios that occur in educational settings.

Although negligence has been discussed and defined in earlier chapters, it is reaffirmed in this chapter because of its crucial importance to the larger issues of safety.

Duty. If the principal is in a grocery store on Saturday afternoon and sees that two of his students are fighting in the middle of the store, the principal has no duty to intervene. Most administrators, however, would intervene from concern for the students and for the reputation of the school or program. Once intervention begins, a person has a duty.

An often-quoted, allegedly apocryphal law school case scenario involves a drowning man and a group of people on the nearby beach who were trying to determine what to do. Finally, one man said that he was a good swimmer and he would save the drowning man. The swimmer began the rescue. When he came within five feet of the man, he realized the man's identity, said, "Oh, it's you," and began swimming back to shore. The law states that once a rescue is attempted, the rescuer must continue unless some extraordinary factor intervenes. This swimmer's action demonstrates that he had assumed the duty of rescue, and, legally, he could not abandon it because of a personal dislike of the individual being rescued.

Violation of duty. It is possible for a duty to exist but not be violated. A real-life example involved a schoolteacher who was riding on a bus transporting students on a field trip. A bee flew into the bus and stung the bus driver. He lost control of the bus and, consequently, some of the students were injured. A group of parents sued the school and alleged that the teacher had violated her duty either by (a) not keeping the bee from flying into the bus, or (b) not keeping the bee from stinging the bus driver. The judge found that the teacher had a duty but that she did not violate it, as the events occurring could hardly have been foreseen.

Proximate cause. The third element needed for a finding of negligence is proximate cause, or a "contributing factor." It involves both commission and omission. If the supervising adult had done what should have been done, there would have been no injury, or if the adult had not done what was done, there would have been no injury. Proximate cause is often referred to as the "but for" connection. "But for" what the teacher did or didn't do, the student would not have been injured.

As discussed in earlier chapters, perhaps the most well-known negligence case in Catholic schools occurred in 1976. A second-grade teacher kept a burning candle on her desk all day to honor the Blessed Mother during the month of May. A child wearing a crepe paper costume walked too close to the flame and was terribly burned. The teacher obviously had no intention of causing harm to anyone, and she herself was badly burned trying to assist the child. The fact remained, however, that "but for" the presence of the candle, the student would not have been injured. Therefore, the requirement of proximate cause was satisfied. This case emphasizes that developing policy dealing with classroom safety issues is at least as important as developing policy dealing with violence in general.

Injury. If no injury resulted from the action of the teacher or other supervisor, there can be no finding of legal negligence, as discussed above. A person can be professionally negligent, even outrageously negligent as described in the drowning incident above, and still avoid legal liability if no injury occurs.

An injury does not have to be physical. Cases alleging mental, emotional, and other injuries have been successfully litigated. A board must plan for the worst-case scenario and cannot afford to simply hope that injuries of any kind will not occur.

Board members share responsibility with the administrator(s) for ensuring that programs and schools are as safe as possible. If a person is injured in such a setting, a claim of negligence will most likely be made. Negligence involves no intent to harm. If intent to harm existed and resulted in an injury, litigation would probably be brought under criminal law charges of assault and battery.

An old adage states: "An ounce of prevention is worth a pound of cure." In a very real sense that adage applies to civil law as it affects educational institutions and programs. Time spent identifying and addressing risks can only aid the operation of the school or program and ensure that the institution is in as legally sound a position as possible.

REFLECTION QUESTIONS

1. The director of religious education has asked the board to appoint a committee to conduct a safety audit of the building. He states that he has no idea how to perform an audit, and asks for some volunteer assistance and some sort of policy statement from the board. How should the board proceed?

2. The school principal has just called you, the board chair. She discovered a small revolver, several boxes of bullets, some dynamite, and a two page "hit" list of intended victims in a student locker. The occupant of the locker has been arrested. The principal wants to know if she needs to notify all the parents of students on the "hit" list and/or all parents in the school. If she does notify either or both groups, should she identify the perpetrator's name? She is worried because some parents claim they cannot protect their children if they do not know who is making the threat. What should the board advise her to do?

19

Some Concluding
Thoughts

C atholic education board members should familiarize themselves
with the law as it affects both private and public education.
Since board members are responsible for the development of policies,
familiarity with the law will be most helpful. Board members should
be cognizant of the principles of law involved in landmark court
decisions and should be able to understand the courts' reasoning. In
so doing, board members will be able to apply the appropriate
concepts to their own policy making.

Although Catholic schools and programs are not bound by all
the constraints that public ones are, knowledge of those constraints
should aid the member in developing policies that are fair and
equitable. Just because an institution is not legally bound to do
something does not mean that the thing should not be done if it
seems the morally right thing to do. Catholic education boards
should always be concerned with respecting the dignity of principals,
DREs, teachers, other school employees, parents, and students as
human beings. This chapter will briefly review the significant areas
of torts, handbooks, and due process.

TORTS

As discussed earlier, the law of torts is basically the same for
private and public institutions. Certainly one of the best recommendations that could be made to board members is to strive always to
act in a manner that is respectful of the dignity, rights, and safety
of all those in the parish and/or school.

Negligence. Since most torts arising in schools are negligence cases, boards should develop clear policies regarding safety and supervision. One major potential safety and supervision area to be addressed by school boards is the use of buildings and grounds. Students present in school buildings and on school or parish grounds without adult supervision is a lawsuit waiting to happen. Court decisions, some 30 years old, indicate that institutions can be held responsible for accidents on playgrounds before and after school or programs. Some schools or programs have policies stating that children are not to arrive before a specified time and are to leave by a certain time, but this rule often is not enforced. No one wants to be insensitive to the problems of working parents. It is not fair, however, for parents to assume that it is permissible to drop children at school very early in the morning and/or to pick them up very late in the afternoon. It is also unfair to assume that teachers or catechists who arrive before they are required to be present or who stay late will be responsible for children. Finally, it is not fair to assume that the principal or other administrator can watch children who arrive early or remain until six or seven o'clock at night. If a child is injured while on school or parish property during an unsupervised time, a court will look at the parent/student handbook to see if a policy is in place and if it has been enforced.

Athletic policies pose supervision problems as well. In some parishes students who do not attend the parish school can play on the team. In effect, this means that it is not a school team but rather a parish team. The pastor and the board cannot expect the principal to be responsible for the supervision of team members from the time school is dismissed until practice begins and/or the coach arrives. If the team is school-sponsored, the problem is really the school board's and the pastor's. If it is a parish team, it may be the parish council's and the pastor's. In any case, the board certainly can develop policy and recommend its implementation to the appropriate parties. Several approaches are possible to this supervision problem. One is to post "no trespassing" signs and enforce a policy of no presence on school or parish property outside specified times. If a student is on the grounds at a time when no supervision is provided, the parents should be notified. Appropriate warnings and penalties should be given. The board might want to consider a policy that would require parents to withdraw a child from school or programs after repeated offenses.

There are, of course, many other options. The important point is to do something. Boards should not take refuge in the belief that since nothing has ever happened, nothing ever will happen. A single lawsuit could be very costly and perhaps could be avoided if policies and procedures are developed and enforced.

Defamation. In this day of increasing litigation, it is good for a board member to consider the risks of being charged with defamation. For instance, board members, especially chairpersons, are often asked to write recommendations for departing teachers and/or principals. People are generally familiar with the problems of writing legally noncontroversial recommendations for persons without sacrificing the truth.

No person has an absolute right to a recommendation, and board members may legitimately refuse a request for a recommendation. Boards should guard against making "deals" with employees who have not met job expectations. Too often, resignations are given in exchange for good recommendations. If the board would not reemploy the person, it is not just to pass problem employees on to another school. A letter verifying employment and stating duties could be given as an alternative.

The guideline is, of course, to be as fair as possible. Board members should strive to be fair and respectful of the dignity of others in all communications (whether official or not) and to be sure that what is said can be shown to have some valid relationship to the professional situation.

POLICY DEVELOPMENT

The beginning point for policy development should be the school's or program's philosophy. Every school/program should have a clearly written philosophy that is available to teachers, parents, and as far as possible, to students. Even very young children can be brought to some understanding of philosophy: "At our school we try to treat each other the way Jesus would want us to treat each other." The life of the school should be seen as flowing from the philosophy.

The school board should annually review all faculty, parent, student, and/or parent/student handbooks as a matter of policy. If policies are clearly written, the likelihood that serious problems will arise is lessened. The board's acceptance of handbooks, which contain rules and regulations as well as policies, will strengthen the positions of both the administrator and the board.

Every school/program should have some sort of written student handbook, even if it is only a few pages in length. School boards might consider having parents and students sign a form stating they have read and/or discussed the rules and agree to abide by them. Having a written handbook should encourage the school to strive for clarity in rule making. Periodic evaluation should enable the school to make necessary changes in rules. (Readers may find *School Handbooks*[9] by this author to be helpful. The National Association of Boards of Catholic Education also offers examples of handbooks and policies.)

When considering the development of policies, board members and administrators must be aware that there is a time investment involved. A person must be allowed to tell his or her side of the story, and education personnel are committed to spending time with people.

Discipline. A discipline example will illustrate. The administrator is committed to listening to the student's side of the story as well as the teacher's in matters of student discipline. The benefit should be obvious: students who perceive persons in authority trying to be fair may internalize the values that are modeled. A student who sees an administrator behaving in a manner that is respectful of the dignity of students may be more likely to afford that same respect to others. Board members can certainly think of analogous situations. Certainly, persons in authority in Catholic schools and programs should be acting from a desire to serve in ministry, not from a desire to wield power. Acting in a manner worthy of ministry in Catholic education will ensure that an institution is acting according to "fundamental reasonableness" and, in the case of litigation, will offer a sound defense.

Catholic schools should be committed to give notice and to hold a hearing in any student discipline case. In this way, the school acts in a fair and moral manner. This commitment would mean that the student is told what he or she did wrong and that an opportunity for hearing the student's side of the story be given.

Somewhat more extensive policies and procedures should be developed if the penalty is suspension. One-day suspensions should require that the parents be notified. Longer suspensions should involve written notification specifying the charges and stating the time and place of the disciplinary hearing. Cases in which the possibility of expulsion exists require written notification and a more formal hearing at which the student and his or her parents should be present.

The right of students and teachers to legal counsel in suspension and/or expulsion hearings is a controversial topic, even in the public school. In the private school, the issue is quite complex. Catholic school board members should understand that there is no legal requirement that a private school permit legal counsel for a student or teacher to be present at a hearing. However, if the school grants that privilege to one person, a precedent could be set requiring that all persons in similar situations be allowed the benefit of legal counsel. Obviously, the decision to allow legal counsel in student or teacher disciplinary proceedings in Catholic schools and programs is not an easy one. Board members should weigh the advantages and disadvantages carefully and should consult with legal counsel before developing policy.

Although constitutional due process has not yet been found to apply to private schools and programs (unless the school or program explicitly grants that right to its students), courts do look for fairness in dealings with students. Many experts believe that private institutions should follow minimum due process procedures because of the demands of simple justice. It seems better to practice preventive disciplinary measures in one's rules and procedures than to test their validity in a courtroom.

Discrimination. Since Catholic institutions are bound by antidiscrimination legislation, boards should be sure that policies stating that the school or parish complies with the legislation are in place. Where reasonable accommodation on the part of the school or program would enable a handicapped student or teacher to be present, the school should make that accommodation. In all areas except religion, Catholic schools and programs should not and cannot discriminate without repercussions. These areas are race, color, national origin, sex (unless traditionally a single sex school), disability, and age. Since it is illegal to discriminate against anyone over the age of 40, Catholic schools and programs must be very careful in employment procedures. It is not legal to give preference in hiring to persons on the basis of age, although it is tempting to hire less experienced people who require lower salaries than do the older, more experienced ones. The only exception would be in the case of true financial exigency, when a school or program honestly could not pay the salary of a more experienced, older employee.

The above recommendations may be helpful to Catholic board members and administrators as they attempt to develop, modify, and implement rules and policies. Ultimately, the guiding principle in any development, modification, and/or implementation of policies and/or rules should be the desire to act in a reasonable, moral way consistent with the Gospel, with the school's philosophy, and with the principles of common law.

Common law demands that every individual try to treat every other individual in a fair manner; but even beyond common law, there is a moral imperative in acting fairly.

CONTRACTS

To help achieve fairness, boards should be sure that the employment contract is clear and outlines the specific expectations that the parish or school has for the employee's conduct. Since the courts can view handbooks as an extension of the contract, boards and administrators should strive to establish clear, reasonable rules and policies. In the same way, the board should review the parents' contract with the school or program, found in both the parent or parent/student handbook and the written contract, where applicable. Schools may wish to consider a written contract that spells out the school's responsibilities and obligates the parents to the payment of tuition and to honoring the policies and rules contained in the handbook. Religious education programs and youth ministry programs should state parental obligations in terms of support and participation and should require student adherence to rules and regulations.

DUE PROCESS

Although Catholic schools and programs are not required to follow constitutional due process procedures, much can be learned from the public schools in this area.

The Gospel would seem to demand that at least the minimum requirements of due process be afforded to teachers and students in Catholic schools.

Justice and common sense indicate that administrators and boards in Catholic schools and programs strive towards reasonable fairness, if not towards constitutional due process. The rudiments of due process should be met in any conflict: notice and hearing before an impartial tribunal. The contractual rights of teachers, other employees, parents, and students should be a concern of every Catholic institution. The courts have indicted that private institutions can be held to a standard of fundamental reasonableness, and it is by that standard (as well as the Gospel) that boards and administrators should seek to judge actions, whether or not court action ever becomes a reality.

A FINAL NOTE

When *A Primer on School Law* was published in 1988, violence in schools rarely occurred. Today, it is commonplace. Catholic schools and programs are just as vulnerable as other schools and programs, and boards must deal with these realities through policy development.

The development of private sector law has been slower than the development of public school law. As this book has indicated, however, lawsuits against schools in general and Catholic schools and programs in particular are on the increase. No longer can Catholic schools and programs expect the judicial restraint that kept courts from intervening in the past. Courts are holding all private institutions to a standard of fairness, as well as to the tenets of contracts made with parents and/or students.

Catholic schools and other church-related programs formerly found almost absolute immunity from successful litigation in the doctrine of separation of church and state. Cases arising over the last several years indicate, however, that courts can and will intervene in non-doctrinal aspects of the Catholic institution's operation.

Catholic school and program personnel and board members can no longer afford to be ignorant of the law as it pertains to them and to their institutions. Ignorance can prove costly in terms of money, time, and the failure to model Gospel values. The study of civil law can provide school and program administrators and board members with the knowledge and tools they need to avoid being sued.

Knowledge of civil law not only can help boards avoid lawsuits, it can also help persons be more effective board members. Justice and common sense seem to demand that Catholic education board members, striving to be faithful to the mission and philosophy of their institutions, seek knowledge of the law.

Civil law is a kind of watchdog over the behavior of institutions. In the final analysis, however, each person—board member, pastor, DRE, youth minister, principal, and teacher—has to answer to his or her conscience. Catholic school and program board members have received a great trust. If they possess wider latitude in governing their institutions than do their public school counterparts, it may be that their responsibilities are also greater.

Jesus' command to let the little children come to him and his prohibition of leading them astray may be the best advice that a board member could ponder. Board members and administrators must realize that they guard the spiritual and physical well-being of those entrusted to their care. Fidelity to their own highest principals and to Gospel imperatives should insure that Catholic education boards remain well within the parameters of the law, both divine and human.

Glossary of Terms

BOARD
A board (committee/council/commission) is a body whose members are selected or elected to participate in decision-making in education at the diocesan, regional, inter-parish, or parish level.

BOARD WITH LIMITED JURISDICTION
A board with limited jurisdiction has power limited to certain areas of educational concern. It has final but not total jurisdiction.

CONSULTATIVE
A consultative board is one which cooperates in the policy-making process by formulating and adapting but never enacting policy.[10]

COLLEGIALITY
Collegiality is a sharing of responsibility and authority. In the Catholic Church, bishops have the highest authority within a diocese. Powers may be delegated to other parties, such as boards.

COMMON LAW
Common law is law not created by a legislature. It includes principles of action based on long-established standards of reasonable conduct and on court judgments affirming such standards. It is sometimes called "judge-made law."

COMPELLING STATE INTEREST
Compelling state interest is the overwhelming or serious need for governmental action. The government is said to have a compelling

state interest in anti-discrimination legislation or the equal treatment of all citizens.

CONTRACT
A contract is an agreement between two parties. The essentials of a contract are: 1) mutual assent 2) by legally competent parties 3) for consideration 4) to subject matter that is legal and 5) in a form of agreement that is legal.

CONSENSUS
As distinguished from majority rule, consensus is a model of decision-making in which a board seeks to arrive at a decision that all members can agree to support.

DEFAMATION
Defamation is communication that injures the reputation of another without good reason. Defamation can be either spoken (slander) or written (libel).

DUE PROCESS
Due process is fundamental fairness under the law. There are two types:

> Substantive Due Process: "The constitutional guarantee that no person shall be arbitrarily deprived of his life, liberty or property; the essence of substantive due process is protection from arbitrary unreasonable action." (*Black*, 1281) Substantive due process concerns *what* is done as distinguished from *how* it is done (procedural due process).

> Procedural Due Process: how the process of depriving someone of something is carried out; *how* it is done. The minimum requirements of constitutional due process are *notice* and *hearing* before an *impartial tribunal*.

EXECUTIVE SESSION
An executive session is a closed meeting to which only members of the board are admitted. If the board is discussing the evaluation of the job performance of an employee, such as the principal, that

person may be asked to leave the meeting during the discussion.

FORESEEABILITY
Foreseeability is "the reasonable anticipation that harm or injury is a likely result of acts or omission." (Black, 584) It is not necessary that a person anticipate that a specific injury might result from an action, but only that danger or harm in general might result.

LANDMARK COURT DECISIONS
Landmark court decisions are decisions of major importance. These decisions are often used as part of the judicial reasoning in later decisions.

NEGLIGENCE
Negligence is the absence of the degree of care which a reasonable person would be expected to use in a given situation.

POLICY
A policy is a guide for discretionary action.[11] Policy states *what* is to be done, not *how* it is to be done.

PRIVATE SCHOOL
A private school is a school owned, operated, and financed by a religious community or by a board of trustees.[12]

PROXIMATE CAUSE
Proximate cause is a contributing factor to an injury. The injury was a result or reasonably foreseeable outcome of the action or inaction said to be the proximate cause.

RESPONDEAT SUPERIOR
Respondeat superior is a principle of civil law that requires that a superior be responsible for the actions of subordinates.

STATE ACTION
State action is the presence of the state (government) in an activity to such a degree that the activity may be considered to be that of the government.

TENURE
Tenure is an expectation of continuing employment.

DE FACTO TENURE
De facto tenure is an expectation in fact that employment will continue, in the absence of a formal tenure policy. De facto tenure can result from past practices of an employer or from length of employment.

Notes

1. Mary Angela Shaughnessy, *A Primer on School Law: A Guide for Board Members in Catholic Schools* (Washington, DC: NCEA, 1988).
2. Chief Administrators of Catholic Education/National Association of Boards of Catholic Education, *A Primer on Educational Governance in the Catholic Church*, ed. J. Stephen O'Brien (Washington, DC: NCEA, 1987) p. 27.
3. Ibid., p. 36.
4. Kern Alexander, *School Law* (St. Paul: West, 1980) p. 343.
5. Richard D. Gatti and Daniel J. Gatti, *New Encyclopedic Dictionary of School Law* (West Nyack, NY: Parker, 1983) p. 246.
6. Mary Angela Shaughnessy, *A Primer on School Law: A Guide for Board Members in Catholic Schools* (Washington, DC: NCEA, 1988).
7. Merickel, *The Educator's Rights to Fair Use of Copyrighted Works*, 51st ed. (Law. Rpr. 711, 1989).
8. Thomas M. Batsis, O.Carm., *Crisis Management in Catholic Schools* (Washington, DC: NCEA, 1994).
9. Mary Angela Shaughnessy, *School Handbooks: Some Legal Consideration* (Washington, DC: NCEA, 1989).
10. Chief Administrators of Catholic Education/National Association of Boards of Catholic Education, p. 59.
11. Ibid., p. 61.
12. Ibid.

Bibliography

Alexander, Kern (1980). *School law.* St. Paul: West.

Black, Henry Campbell (1990). *Black's law dictionary.* (6th ed.). St. Paul: West.

Buckley Amendment of 1975.

Chief Administrators of Catholic Education/National Association Boards of Education.

Copyright Act of 1909.

Copyright Act of 1976.

Gatti, Richard D. and Gatti, Daniel J. (1983). *New encyclopedic dictionary of school law.* West Nyack, NY: Parker.

Individuals with Disabilities in Education Act.

Merickel, "The Educator's Right to Fair Use of Copyrighted Works," 51 Ed.Law.Rptr. 711 (1989).

O'Brien, J. Stephen ed. (1987). *A primer on educational governance in the Catholic church.* Washington, DC: National Catholic Educational Association.

Pastoral Statement of U.S. Catholic Bishops on Handicapped People (1988).

Valente, William D. (1980). *Law in the schools.* Columbus: Merrill.